A Taste of Australia: BITE-SIZED TRAVELS ACROSS A SUNBURNED COUNTRY

Alistair McGuinness

Published by Alistair McGuinness, 2020.

A TASTE OF AUSTRALIA: BITE-SIZED TRAVELS ACROSS A SUNBURNED COUNTRY

First edition. November 30, 2020.

Written by Alistair McGuinness.

Daydream Believer

"Believe in your dreams. They were given to you for a reason."
– Katrina Mayer

With three brothers, one sister and a crazy dog called Barney, there was rarely a dull moment in my childhood home. We grew up in a three-bedroom rental, overlooked by an expanse of trampled grass frequented by dog walkers and boisterous kids, playing football each weekend while using jumpers as goalposts.

Each summer, Mum and Dad would drive us across England and Wales, to board a ferry for Ireland, before travelling north and west to County Donegal, renowned for its charming villages, misty hills and wild, untamed coastline. Throughout the long journey, we'd take unplanned diversions, as Mum struggled with the map and Dad muttered at the wheel.

For two weeks, we'd stay with my grandmother in the house where she once raised 15 children. On special evenings, I'd sit with a fizzy drink in one of the local pubs, listening to tales from long ago as my great uncles, Barney and Francie, enthralled visitors with their recitations of life in rural Donegal. Each was an Irish storyteller, known as a Seanchaí, and they'd take it in turns to stand proudly by the bar, cloth cap in hand while spinning yarns to smiling patrons sipping on Guinness.

After listening to Barney and Francie, my mind raced with thoughts about one day having the confidence to tell inspiring or humorous stories to strangers. These aspirations stayed with me throughout my teenage years, as I'd stare from my bedroom window at the lights of the airport tower, daydreaming about travelling far and wide.

Fast forward forty years and so much has changed. Somewhere during this time, the awkward shyness slipped away, replaced by a curiosity to see the world. This led to adventures and escapades through parts of South America, Africa and Australia with my wife, Fran. We now live in Australia with our two teenage boys, and a dog called Peppi, who is far gentler than my childhood pet, renowned for patrolling the streets for soft targets until taken to the compound, never to return!

Since moving from England, I've taken every opportunity to explore this vast, sunburned country and now have an abundance of travel stories to share. I often wonder what my great uncles would have thought about Australia. One thing for sure, they'd have found a cosy pub somewhere on their travels, maybe in one of the dusty outback towns, where nomads, prospectors and locals congregate each day to escape the heat.

Although Barney and Francie are no longer around to tell their stories, I'm happy to follow in their footsteps. I cannot play the fiddle like they used to and do not have a soft Irish lilt, but within these pages there is a sprinkle of humour along with a selection of maps to help guide you. Along the way, you'll discover the extremes of Australia, from close encounters with venomous snakes, to the serenity of posing for a selfie alongside the cutest, most adorable creature on planet earth—the quokka!

Australia cannot be defined in one sentence or story. It is a place of mystery and diversity, from the searing outback to the frozen peaks of the Snowy Mountains. The country has been inhabited for over 60,000 years and there is much to learn from the original custodians. I've enjoyed excursions with Aboriginal guides, heading into the wilderness, searching for bushtucker while listening to stories passed down by generations.

Now it's my turn to tell a few stories, including a climb to the top of Sydney Harbour Bridge, followed by escapades stretching from the outback to Tasmania and across the Nullarbor Plain to Western Australia. So, grab a refreshing drink and find a shady spot before turning the next page. We're about to take a bumpy ride!

Riders on the Storm

"Don't worry about the world coming to an end today. It is already tomorrow in Australia."
– Charles M. Schulz

'Alistair, have you seen the news? You need to come quickly.'

While searching through my wardrobe, I heard my wife call out again. 'Where are you, Ali? I need you to see this.'

'One second, Fran, I'm just looking for my Donegal—'

'I don't think you'll need to pack anything, especially the shirt you bought in Ireland. There's no way you'll be flying to work on Saint Patrick's Day.'

Moments later, I was standing in front of our TV, staring at the satellite image on the screen. Out to sea, far to the north of the state, a large storm had formed between the islands of Indonesia. Most of the archipelago was hidden from view by a swirling mass of inky clouds. The circles in the centre were bunched together, but the clouds at the edges had trailed away, as if to reach out and touch the shores of Western Australia. I turned up the volume, just in time to hear the final snippet from the reporter.

'*It looks to be gathering strength while travelling south across the Timor Sea and has now been classified as a severe tropical cyclone. As with all cyclones, this one also has a name. Cyclone Lua is due to make landfall within a few hours, before moving inland towards—*'

Fran hit the mute button and turned to face me. 'That storm is heading towards the Pilbara. You can't fly north in the morning–straight into the path of a cyclone. Have you checked your work emails? Surely your flight has been cancelled.'

I dismissed her concerns with a shrug of the shoulders, hoping she wouldn't see how spooked I'd become at the sight of the satellite image. We'd moved to Australia in search of an adventure or two, and it looked like I was about to get my fair share in the next 48 hours.

With my back turned, I made my way to the kitchen and called out, 'I checked earlier and at the moment it's all systems go. I'm sure they'll postpone my flight, but I've got to be ready, just in case the storm changes direction or fizzles out. With luck, they'll cancel the flight and put me up in a fancy hotel for the night. This time tomorrow I could be lounging by an outdoor pool—'

Fran came up close and put her hand on mine. 'Or you could be in a remote mine site that's been ravaged by a cyclone, or worse still...'

While she shared her thoughts, I eased out a smile and clicked the kettle on. 'Well, let's wait and see. I've got one more day at home before I need to go anywhere, so at least we can enjoy a cup of tea together first.'

Later that day, I checked on the internet to find the most up-to-date satellite image. As predicted by the weather bureau, the cyclone had continued to track south. Although I could see the outline of Western Australia, the rest of the image told a different story. Beyond the northern tip of the country, there was nothing to see except dappled clouds, whipped together in an angry swathe across the Timor Sea.

A link below the image directed me to another website, where I quickly learned about the previous cyclones that have struck Australia. The list was extensive and included one or two storms that had left death and destruction in their wake. With this sobering thought, I then checked my work emails for the umpteenth time. There was no change. I needed to check in at Perth airport the following morning by 5.30 a.m.

That evening, I kissed Fran and our children goodnight before making my way to the spare room, hoping that by the time

I woke, the flight would have been postponed. Six hours later, I sat up, rubbed my eyes and checked for any recent updates. There was still no change.

After a two-minute shower, I dressed in a fluorescent work shirt, jeans and steel toe-capped boots, in readiness for a day of work on the mines. Balancing tea and toast, I then crept out of the house and threw my holdall onto the back seat of the car for the three-hour trip. I had the roads and highway to myself for the first part of the journey but remained vigilant for kangaroos bounding out of the darkness into the full beam of my weary Suzuki. By the time I caught sight of the control tower at Perth airport, the sky was changing colour, with the promise of another warm day for the residents.

Despite the early hour, the approach road was busy, with hundreds of other Fly-In-Fly-Out miners in transit to the terminal. Just like me, they were leaving behind friends and family for another roster in the far north. As each driver searched for a vacant space in the crowded car park, I wondered if they were all thinking the same as me? *Surely the flights heading north will be cancelled for the day.*

While at the check-in desk, I overheard two burly miners, who were in conversation at the adjacent console. 'Do you reckon our flight will go ahead? It's looking crazy up north at the moment.'

The other man shrugged and said, 'We won't be flying anywhere today–you mark my words. In a few hours, we'll be back at home, on full pay.'

On the way to the boarding gate, I stopped to study a widescreen TV. Cyclone Lua dominated the screen, its darkened swirls fast approaching the shores of Western Australia. I kept walking towards the gate, waiting for the overhead announcement that would turn each passenger back.

Twenty minutes later I was buckled into a window seat, alongside a miner who'd dressed in anticipation of a hard day's work, just like every other passenger on board. Compared to my bright fluorescent shirt, his looked worn and faded and I wondered how many years he'd worked on the mines, flying to and from work each week. His eyes were hidden behind sunglasses, so there was no way of knowing if he was awake as the captain's reassuring voice resonated throughout the cabin, welcoming us on board.

The next voice on the intercom belonged to the first officer. After a quick introduction, he then set the scene for the next few hours.

'Once airborne, those of you seated on the left will get the chance to enjoy fine views of the city as it wakes, plus Rottnest Island, just offshore. We'll then head north along the coast before turning inland. Strong winds are forecast, which could mean we are in for a bumpy ride. Please keep your seat belts fastened throughout the flight, in case we encounter turbulence along the way.'

After he'd signed off, I gained the attention of one of the flight crew, a dark-haired woman who I guessed to be in her early thirties. Despite the early hour, she looked bright eyed, without a single crease in her royal blue uniform. Her eyes continually darted between nearby passengers, as she stood close by, waiting for me to talk. I raised my voice above the sound of the high-pitched engines and called out, 'Do you think we'll be able to land at the mine site if the weather is as bad as they say?'

In reply, she produced a professional smile and stepped a little nearer. 'The weather in the Pilbara is holding up, so I think we'll be fine. I hope you enjoy the flight.'

And with that, she turned her attention to a nearby miner, slouched low in his seat. She gently prodded him to attention, then asked him to buckle his seat belt. A few minutes later we were in the air, and as promised by the first officer, I got the chance to enjoy a bird's-eye view of the city, followed by the opportunity to spot cargo ships on their way to Fremantle Harbour.

Despite the glint of sunlight on the ocean and the faraway sighting of the low-lying island of Rottnest, I couldn't quite appreciate the beauty. Instead, my mind whirred with unanswered questions.

Why are we flying towards an area that is about to be pounded by a cyclone?

Will the plane turn around at any second, with an apology from the captain saying that it was all a mistake?

Why am I the only one on board who seems to be agitated?

Will I get the chance to raise a glass of Guinness this evening, in memory of my mum?

As I gazed out of the window, the plane continued to climb while veering northeast, away from the coastline. Moments later, the ocean view disappeared, replaced by a menacing blanket of murky clouds. I glanced around the cabin at the other passengers, hoping for reassurance from a friendly face, but most on board had their eyes shut. We'd already been advised there'd be no refreshments served, because of the risk of turbulence.

With nothing to look forward to apart from a rough ride ahead, followed by a close encounter with a cyclone, I followed suit and closed my eyes. Seconds later they popped open, as the plane bounced around in a crosswind, as though we were in a fairground car, being bumped from all sides. While gripping the armrests, I peered outside to see if we were still climbing, but there was no sunlight, just a shroud of dark clouds surrounding the aircraft.

Despite the bumps, jolts and sudden drops which turned my stomach, the miner to my right didn't flinch throughout the flight. He remained still and silent, with his legs stretched under the seat in front. Maybe he'd been through this scenario before, but for me this was a novel experience. While living in England, I'd had the luxury of being able to commute to work by bicycle whenever I took the notion, especially in the warmer months.

Before moving to Australia, I'd rarely encountered anyone who travelled to work by plane each week. I'd always considered that type of commute to be for movie stars or millionaires. But Australia is a vast country, and most of its iron ore reserves are found in remote areas, far from major towns and cities. To extract the ore, thousands of workers are flown out to the mines to work for long periods of time.

The next intercom announcement took me by surprise, as I must have dozed off. '*Cabin crew, please prepare for landing.*'

I peered outside, expecting to see the vibrant red landscape that makes the Pilbara so appealing. Once again, there was nothing but streaks of rain on the window and dappled clouds that gave few clues about how low we were. I then felt the plane make a shallow turn, as we continued to descend.

As each minute passed, I willed the clouds to depart, but they remained as dark and creamy as the Guinness I'd planned to enjoy later that evening. I then decided that if anyone needed the luck of the Irish, it had to be the pilot. Down there, hidden in the mist was a single strip of tarmac, and with every second we were getting closer.

By now, even the miner next to me had stirred to life. He removed his sunglasses, leaned over and studied the scene outside. 'Be a close one, I reckon.'

Then he returned to his seat and closed his eyes once more. What did he mean by *a close one*? I wanted to tap him on the shoulder and ask, but a sudden thought struck me. Maybe the captain was about to abort the landing. Any second now, we'd be pushed into our seats as the aircraft changed direction, soaring higher before looping round and heading back to Perth.

These thoughts diminished in an instant, as a flash of light outside the window grabbed my attention. Moments later, we popped out of the clouds to the sound of the wheels being lowered from the undercarriage. The sky above was iron grey and the ground below looked close enough to touch. If this had been my first-ever encounter with the Pilbara, I'd have been disappointed. Instead of a landscape of sunburned red, entwined with spinifex and gum trees, a damp and foreboding country loomed into view.

The plane banked to the left and continued to descend, startling a lone kangaroo. For a few seconds I watched it in action, bouncing across the wet ground towards distant trees. I then spotted a scattering of buildings as we approached the airfield. The pilot banked one more time, allowing me the chance to observe the windsock, blowing hard towards the runway. Just before landing, the aircraft's wings see-sawed from left to right, as the pilot fought against a crosswind. Then there was a bump, followed by a skid, and we were down. Seconds later, the engines were switched into reverse thrust, as the end of the runway drew closer.

While disembarking, I met the stewardess whom I'd chatted with earlier. She smiled once again and said, 'I think we made it just in time. Mind you, I need to get the next passengers on board as quickly as possible, as the weather is closing in.'

And with that, she wished me good luck and watched as I went down the steps towards the red dirt. While walking towards the perimeter fence, I caught sight of a long line of people, all waiting to board the same plane that I'd just travelled on. Some had just completed their seventh night shift in a row and would be yearning to escape the clutches of the storm, with the chance to grab some rest during the flight home. Weary faces with tired eyes studied the plane, waiting for the signal to board as I passed them by in search of my luggage.

While I waited alongside other miners for a minibus to take us to camp, the plane began filling with the outgoing work crew. It then headed to the far end of the runway and turned half circle. Through the window of the minibus, I watched it hurtle down the runway, before lifting into the sky. Within seconds, it had vanished from sight. In its place were darkening clouds, gathering strength.

We were dropped off outside the tavern, but the shutters were down, and would stay that way until the all clear was given. Even though it was Saint Patrick's Day, there would be no Guinness for me, or cold beers for the miners tonight! I studied the scene and tried counting the number of workers packed together in the undercover area. There were at least two hundred of us, all waiting for instructions.

A burst of rainfall on the tin roof threatened to drown out the welcome speech from the safety superintendent who'd stepped onto a wooden bench to address the crowd. He raised his voice and tried again. 'Okay everyone, please listen up. The night shift got out on the last flight, which is brilliant news for them. We are now in a lockdown, because of a severe weather system that is on its way. At this stage we have been advised that it will be a category two cyclone, but we are not taking any chances, as it could grow stronger.'

He stopped for a moment to answer a few questions and then continued. 'The pool, gym and tavern are closed until further notice. Please make your way to your rooms and remain there until you hear the all-clear siren. Don't forget to take enough food to last until the morning at least. If we find anyone wandering around camp after midday, they'll need an excellent reason and will probably have earned a window seat on the next available flight. For those of you that are new to mining, this means we will escort them from site, never to return.'

After the speech, I lined up for my share of provisions and overheard two friends in animated discussion about the weather. They'd come prepared, with movies to watch on their laptops and magazines to read if the lockdown went on for longer than expected. One had been working up north during a previous cyclone and described an incident he'd heard about. 'The bloke in the room next door couldn't go through the night without a smoke. Just after sunset he stepped outside to light up, thinking no one would spot him. It was blowing like crazy and everyone was bunkered down, so he wouldn't have been spotted. But his door slammed shut, and he'd left his key behind. He had to trudge through the wind and rain in search of the security hut. As soon as the storm cleared, he was escorted from site and given a window seat on the next flight. I never saw him again.'

I left the miners to their stories and headed to my cabin, loaded down with sandwiches, fruit, biscuits and water, in readiness for the storm. Sometime after nightfall the power went out, but I'd already been warned about leaving the cabin to investigate. To do so could cost me my life and if caught by a security guard, would likely cost me my job. As the storm raged outside, I climbed into my single bed and pulled the covers up tight. For a while I lay perfectly still, listening to the wind as it howled like an out-of-control freight train, thundering down the track.

By midnight I was still wide awake and for a fleeting moment contemplated getting out of bed to witness the scene outside. But the thought of having the door ripped from its hinges by a freak gust of wind, while I stood in the doorway dressed in a Donegal shirt and boxer shorts, soon brought me back to my senses.

Instead, I reached for my phone, selected a playlist and slipped on my headphones. As the first song came to life, the wind outside died away, replaced by the harmonious sound of Chris Martin from Coldplay. Kings of Leon came next, followed by Snow Patrol and Oasis.

The last track I heard came from The Doors, and as the haunting melody of *Riders on the Storm* filled my ears, I felt the night slip away. Just as sleep beckoned, I tried remembering all the events that had brought me from a suburban street in England to the edge of the West Australian desert, during the middle of a cyclone.

Fork in the Road

"Don't wait. Life goes faster than you think."
– Unknown

While growing up as a teenager in England, my family often described me as a daydreamer. I was also a shy boy, especially compared with my three boisterous brothers, David, Michael and Matthew, who seemed to be forever in and out of the house. Our sister, Alice, was the unsung warrior who helped shepherd us through the storm when Mum and Dad decided to split.

During the long chilly winter nights, I'd often sit by the warmth of my bedroom radiator, while staring out at the darkened streets, wondering what life had in store for me. In the warmer months, the windows would be opened wide, allowing me to listen to the roar of distant jet engines. Beyond the housing estates and industrial units stood Luton Airport, just 30 miles north of London. Although small compared with Heathrow, the airport connected my hometown with many European hotspots, and each year another country or sun-drenched isle seemed to be added to the growing list of destinations.

As each plane appeared in the evening sky, I'd stare at the red taillights and dream about the day that it would be my turn to travel far and wide, conjuring up exciting images of me on top of some faraway mountain, or on the deck of a sailing ship, heading into the sunset. Maybe one day I'd board a flight from

London to Lima or take a train ride across the Canadian Rockies.

By my early twenties, it finally dawned on me I'd achieved none of those dreams! Instead, I'd buckled down to complete a four-year electrical apprenticeship involving night school, college tuition and long days at work. While on this roller-coaster journey, the shyness fell away, to be replaced by an inquisitive and chatty nature, as if making up for lost time!

With a newfound confidence and an electrical trade under my belt, I began setting my sights on a trip to Australia. The family-run business where I worked was between contracts and the time seemed perfect to hand in my cards.

My plan was to spend six months in Australia–to drive along the east coast in a campervan–to explore the outback, to learn to surf at Bondi Beach, to stand on the top of Sydney Harbour Bridge and to experience the people and the places, while soaking up the sunshine.

Then one day, my dad handed me the local newspaper and pointed to an advert near the back pages. The largest employer in the town, Vauxhall Motors, was after a maintenance electrician. I didn't need my dad to tell me that this was a rare event. Very few employees ever left Vauxhall before retirement, and for good reason. They paid decent wages, and the excellent working conditions included three weeks paid holiday per year. During the successful interview, I also learned that they'd send me to university to further my studies.

Suddenly, I faced two choices. I could follow my childhood dream and take to the open road, with my sights set on Australia. Or I could follow my dad's advice and join a company that was owned by General Motors, one of the largest organisations in the world. I decided to join Vauxhall, but vowed to leave after three or four years. My plan was to work hard, learn heaps of new skills, gain further qualifications, save like crazy and *then* head to Australia.

The job required me to help maintain the automated machines that welded the bodywork of each new car together. Sometimes this meant programming industrial robots or fixing faults on overhead conveyors. Night shifts were calmer and less technical. When possible, I stole away from the workshop to complete my studies, or to sit with colleagues and play card games.

All of this sounded perfect, except I was still determined to explore the world. A few years after starting at Vauxhall, I took the plunge and moved into a two-bedroom terraced house near the town centre. I now had a hefty monthly mortgage to pay, which meant deferring the day that I'd travel to Australia for the epic trip I'd always promised myself.

While many of my workmates continued to climb the property ladder, I remained in the same cramped house, in an area of town that seemed to be forever in decline. The only things I wanted to climb were the craggy peaks of the Lake District or the wild and windswept mountains of Scotland. These ambitions led me to the frozen summit of Mont Blanc, the highest peak in Western Europe.

For my first long-haul trip, I ventured to Africa with a friend. We booked a trip on board an overland truck, which would take us into the heart of the Serengeti National Park, for the chance to witness one of the greatest wildlife spectacles on earth–the wildebeest migration.

After the safari, we planned to climb Kilimanjaro, the highest peak in Africa. We'd spend the last week in Mombasa, learning to scuba dive in the Indian Ocean. I'd need 22 days off in a row and would return to Heathrow Airport three hours before my night shift started.

I still remember the moment I put in my holiday request. In those days, it needed to be handwritten on a form, which I then gave to my foreman. Geoff was old school—straight down the line. He could see through most charades and appreciated those who put in a good day's work. As he picked up my holiday slip and began reading the dates, his head slowly shook from side to side. 'Alistair, you haven't got enough holiday banked up for all of this.'

I'd been waiting for such a reply and smiled across the desk at him. 'Not yet, Geoff, but I'm close. I worked during the whole of Easter and haven't received my days in lieu yet. My holiday isn't for another few months and within that time I'll have accrued another three days. Plus, I'm on nights when I arrive back and won't need to put in a holiday for the Monday.'

He eased out a smile and signed the paperwork while muttering to himself about my relentless passion to travel. Just as I was about to leave his office, he called out, 'Alistair, where are you heading to this time?'

'I'm off to Africa, to climb the highest freestanding mountain in the world. Before that, I'm going on a safari. I can't afford to stay in a lodge, so I'm going camping for a few nights in the Serengeti.'

His eyes widened as he studied me by the doorway, dressed in worn overalls, while holding a test meter and screwdriver. 'Did you just say you're going to Africa—on a safari! In case you've forgotten, you work as an electrician in a car factory. I'd love to know how you manage to pay for such extravagant holidays each year. Why don't you just go to Spain or Greece, like the rest of us?'

As I walked away smiling, I thought back to Geoff's comments. He knew I worked overtime most weekends to save for these big trips. I had nothing against Spain or any of the Greek islands and had often enjoyed week-long holidays in the sun with friends, lapping up the nightlife. But I now craved something more than a packaged holiday that offered cheap drinks, mediocre excursions and the chance of a suntan.

The trip to Africa went well, apart from the fact that all my possessions were stolen the day before the climb began. I ended up wearing borrowed pink tracksuit pants and a baggy woollen jumper during my time on the mountain. Unfortunately, my bid for the summit faltered on the last morning, because of severe altitude sickness! Regrettably, I had to be escorted from the snow lined crater rim towards safety, despite being so close to the top.

A week after touching the snows of Kilimanjaro I dropped my rucksack onto the workshop floor, changed into my overalls and clocked on for another night shift. During the midnight break, one of my workmates asked where I'd been for the last three weeks. I mentioned about the overland truck heading across Kenya and Tanzania and explained about the robbery. I also let him know what it was like to sleep in a flimsy tent, with wild lions prowling outside, while in the middle of an African game reserve.

His reply took me by surprise. 'Why do you waste so much time and money on travel? I've just moved to a new house for the third time in seven years and have now got a four-bedroom detached on the edge of town. You could do the same if you wanted.'

'Bert,' I said, 'I'm glad for you. But that's your dream, not mine. For me, life is about travelling far and wide. I'd like each trip to last far longer, but I also enjoy my job and am not ready to pack it all in just yet.'

In reply, he asked, 'Where in the world would you like to explore, if you had more time and money?'

The answer was simple. 'Australia has been on my mind for years, but I think a country like that needs months, not weeks, to explore. And there is no way that will happen, not unless I leave Vauxhall.'

Then, as life is prone to do, the years slipped past. Thirteen years later I was still commuting to the same factory, along with tens of thousands of others, including Bert. During this period, I fell in and out of love, until one day I fell into the arms of a bubbly blonde girl called Fran, while attending a gym class.

I soon learned that she spoke fluent Romanian, after spending two years there as a volunteer in the orphanages. She'd also done something that I was still hoping to do. She'd travelled across most of Australia and had fallen in love with the wide-open spaces and sense of freedom. As for going back again, she was very keen. The timing just had to be right for the return trip!

As our relationship blossomed, we began travelling together, including trips to New York and the Alps. Then one morning I blindfolded Fran and drove her to a mystery location. A few hours later she was sitting beside me, on a flight from London to the land of fire and ice. We were heading to Iceland for a whirlwind day trip. Partway through the day, we stripped to our bathers and soaked in the warm turquoise waters of the Blue Lagoon.

In this tranquil setting, with mountains as a backdrop and pockets of steam drifting past, the time seemed right for me to propose. After we'd swum to the edge of the lagoon, I dropped to one knee and popped the question!

Luckily for me, she said yes, and by the time we'd married, I'd replaced my overalls with a shirt and tie, and started a new role within Vauxhall as a Planning Engineer. Throughout this time, Australia never made it to the top of our travel list, maybe because we wanted more than three weeks to explore it all.

By the time I'd reached the tender age of 37, all thoughts of an extensive trip around Australia had vanished. The only holiday in the pipeline was a Christmas getaway to the Lake District National Park with Fran. With luck, we'd get the chance to walk across the snowy peaks, before enjoying a meal and drinks by an open fire in one of the village pubs.

In the New Year, we planned to move out of our hometown, into a semi-detached house in a nearby village. But on a wet and windy Tuesday in early December, fate seemed to have other plans for us. Without knowing it, our lives were about to change just after midday!

With no prior warning, Vauxhall Motors announced to the media that it was closing down their car manufacturing plant at Luton. This information made the lunchtime headlines on British TV. Within minutes, the scene on the production lines changed from midweek humdrum to shock and confusion, as the news spread like wildfire throughout the factory. After nearly 100 years of operation, the end was nigh.

As angry and confused workers stormed across the factory floor in search of answers, I stood and watched the heartbreaking spectacle. Throughout the commotion, my mind whirred with thoughts:

I'm about to lose my job.

My career is at an end.

I need to call my wife.

We're about to move into a house in the countryside–what will happen now?

Then, out of the blue, another thought came to mind. It wasn't a new one–in fact it had been hibernating in the far reaches of my mind for many years.

Maybe this is finally the time to travel around Australia.

Three hours after the shocking announcement, I found myself in a crowded backstreet pub called Maggie's Bar, contemplating the news. Somewhere in the corner, my nephew was sitting on a stool, guitar on lap, belting out requests for the bewildered workers.

Some of those around me looked to be in a daze. Others seemed at ease, with raised beers in hand, debating whether to march with the unions or take a payout and get on with the rest of their lives. The government had already commented on the announcement, with assurances the factory would remain open for at least another year.

While those around me discussed their future, I sat alongside them, thinking about the chance to travel around Australia. During a lull in the conversation, I detoured towards a quiet corner of the pub, took a deep breath and called my wife. 'Hi Fran, are you sitting down?'

'That's a funny question. Is everything okay?'

'Well, yes–and no.'

'What is that supposed to mean? Is something wrong?'

'Well, I have good news and some not so good news.'

'Just give me the bad news first. By the way–where are you and what's all that noise in the background?'

'I'm in Maggie's Bar—'

'But you're supposed to be at work. It's only—'

'That's the bad news. As I've just—'

'Don't tell me they've sacked you. What did you—'

'I haven't done anything wrong. None of us have, but it looks like we're all about to lose our jobs.'

'What are you on about? Do you mean you and your team?'

'No, it will affect every single employee. General Motors is planning to close some of their factories across the world, including the car plant at Luton.'

'Have you been drinking, Ali? Is this a joke? If so, it's just not funny. We're going to view a house in the countryside this weekend in case you'd forgotten.'

'How would you feel if we didn't go?'

'What are you on about? We've planned it for weeks and the estate agent reckons the house is priced to sell. This is finally our time to move to a country village. Please stop the jokes and come home.'

'This isn't a joke! It's real and scary and lots of people went nuts today. Some thrashed their work stations and others stormed the director's office, demanding answers. The announcement came right out of the blue, but I've heard they're keeping the factory running for another year. This will give me some time to save. I'll also get a payout–plus lots of time off at the end.'

'Of course you'll get plenty of time off–you won't have a job anymore,' Fran reminded me down the line.

'Very true, but the payout might be enough to take us to Australia. You've always said you wanted to go back, and I've been dreaming about the place for years. Hopefully, I've got the right skills and experience to secure a permanent visa.'

The reality of my suggestion suddenly hit home, as Fran replied in an instant. 'Australia–you want to move to Australia? Is this the good news you promised?'

'Yes, I think the time is right for both of us. I can feel it in my bones. I've enjoyed listening about your adventures in Byron Bay and Sydney. Maybe we could—'

'Ali, that was 15 years ago! Yes, it was magical, and I never wanted to leave, but I'm happy in England. I'm not leaving my mum and dad to move to Australia and in case you've forgotten we're meant to be moving to the countryside.'

While I contemplated a worthy reply, she set off again. 'What about your dad? He's getting older and you get on so well. I'm glad I did all those things when I was younger and now there's the chance for us to live in a village, just like we talked about on our wedding day. Pretty soon we'll have chickens and can start planning for the day we get a Vietnamese pot-bellied pig.'

'Fran, I want all those things too. But I also want to experience some of what you did in Australia. My dad travelled the world when he was young and if we stay in Australia, he'd love to visit. Don't you see? I can finally go, which means *we* can have a proper adventure together. If we save hard in the next year and stick to a budget, our trip could last for six months. If we get a permanent visa, we could stay for as long as we like.'

The line fell silent, so I asked, 'Did you hear all that? What do you think?'

Fran's voice was barely a whisper. 'We both know that I've always wanted to go back to Australia, but this is all too sudden for my liking. We're so close to our dream move and suddenly you want to give it all up.'

Then she said something I wasn't prepared for. 'I think you're in shock. You know, because of the announcement about the factory. Why don't you come home so we can talk it through?'

My answer was louder than it needed to be and came from somewhere deep in my subconscious. 'Fran, I've never been more serious in all my life! I just know this is meant to be for both of us. A year from now, we could be driving down the west coast of Australia, with a surfboard on the roof rack and the wind in our hair. You won't even be thinking about a cottage in the English countryside.'

'Ali, you're nearly 40 and haven't even got any hair. Why didn't you take a few months off work when you were in your twenties or thirties? We've only been married a few years, and it's finally coming together. What about our plans to start a...'

While Fran shared her feelings, I let my mind wander. This was one of those moments when I'd reached a crossroads in my life. It's just that I hadn't expected it that morning when I got up for work and drove in the rain towards the factory.

Now I was standing in a packed pub, considering the fork in the road that I'd suddenly arrived at. One way would mean a life in the countryside and the hefty mortgage payments that went with it. I'd have to find a new job, maybe with the sister company next door, which made vans instead of cars. If General Motors continued to keep that factory open, I'd be set for the next 25 years!

Maybe we'd go on a worldwide cruise after my retirement, and then travel along the east coast of Australia in an air-conditioned luxury coach, complete with a tour guide. Somehow, it all seemed too long away and far less appealing.

When at last she stopped talking, I took a deep breath and gave it one more try. 'Fran, there will always be houses in the countryside for sale. And as for the other things we want to do, they can happen in any part of the world. This could be our time to travel far and wide together, while still fit and healthy. What do you think?'

As I pressed my ear to the phone, I could hear the emotion in her voice. 'I don't know what to think anymore. I've always loved your spontaneous nature, but I'm overwhelmed right now. Australia sounds appealing. I loved it back then, and I'm sure I'd enjoy it again. But we are so close to moving and my mum would—'

'Your mum and dad could visit anytime. They're retired and love to travel.'

'Ali, I'm not saying no, but can you appreciate that this is all very sudden? We can chat about it in the morning, when you've got a clearer head. Please don't do anything silly this evening, like booking flights or searching for houses in Sydney!'

I ended the call with the promise to keep my emotions in check and headed back to my workmates. By now, some had formed a tight circle and as I inched my way to the front, I heard their animated chat. One or two wanted to leave immediately and forge new careers, away from a life on the factory floor. Many others kept shaking their heads in disbelief, as they tried digesting the news given earlier.

Phil: 'Surely the factory will stay open. If not, the whole town will suffer.'

Jim: 'You better believe it, as we're on the scrapheap.'

Scott: 'I'm moving to the south coast. I've had enough of this town.'

Tony: 'Maybe it's about time I became self-employed.'

Phil: 'You must be joking, mate. You've never done a hard day's work in your life.'

When it came to my turn, I raised my voice above the sound of the music. 'I've just called Fran to tell her the news. I also let slip that I think we should move to Australia, instead of moving to the countryside.'

From the back, someone shouted out, 'I bet she thinks you're mad. Why would you want to move over there, with all those spiders, snakes and man-eating crocodiles?'

Before I could defend the notion of moving to Australia, a barrage of questions came my way.

'Where will you live and work?'

'When are you going?'

'What about the house in the country you've been after?'

I smiled and shook my head, acknowledging that I was heading into the unknown. In the silence that followed, I gave the best answer I could muster. 'I've no idea about where to live and work, but we might find a village or country town on the outskirts—'

The reply from a nearby colleague was not what I expected. 'Australia hasn't got many villages, Alistair. Not like the ones here, with ponds, pubs and post offices. They've got sprawling suburbs in Melbourne and outback towns with little more than a tin shed for a pub and gold prospectors for clientele.'

'How do you know all this?' I asked. 'I didn't know you'd been to Australia.'

'I watched something about it on YouTube once. The place is deadly, I tell you. They have funnel-web spiders that live under toilet seats. One bite and you can say goodbye to your testicles! Plus, they have man-eating crocodiles and venomous snakes...'

I let Gerry continue with his rant, based on information he'd discovered while trawling through YouTube, when he should have been repairing broken lights at the factory!

When at last he stopped for breath, I replied in an instant. 'Maybe you're right, Gerry. But if it's that bad, why do millions of people visit there every year? Yes, I might get my gonads nibbled by a spider and there's always the risk of getting chomped in half by a croc. But I might also learn to surf on the east coast or find a job in a gold mine and get to live by the ocean. Instead of watching *Neighbours* or *Home and Away* on TV, I could be living that kind of lifestyle!'

Then I held a hand up. 'But first I need to listen to Fran. It's a big decision and we have lots to consider. I'm just thankful that her parents enjoy travelling and will be able to visit. Hopefully, my dad can come over too.'

And with that I went in search of a beer, wishing my mum had been alive, as I really needed her advice. She'd moved from Ireland to England in search of a new life, with few regrets. While at the bar, I smiled at the memory of my mum, taken too early by cancer. You only get one chance in life and with this thought I raised my glass, said a quiet prayer and made my way towards the music.

Fran and I never went to see the house in the quaint English village. I heard through a friend that a family of three from London purchased it within weeks. Instead, we opened a bottle of wine that weekend and talked about our dreams and aspirations. Village life was put on hold, in favour of a trip around the world. Our ultimate destination would be Australia and once there, we'd give it a year or two, before returning to England to find a place in the countryside.

Twenty years later, we are still in Australia! It hasn't all been blue skies and barbeques, but there has been more sunshine than rain. We have also had the chance to embrace special moments with visitors from back home, including our parents. Throughout this time, we have enjoyed many bite-sized adventures, sometimes close to home or close to nature, in national parks and remote camping spots.

As the Chinese philosopher, Lao Tzu, once said, *The journey of a thousand miles begins with a single step*. The first step that led me to Australia occurred long ago and I plan to take many more across this vast, sunburned land.

My Hometown

"Sometimes, it's the smallest decisions that can change your life forever."
– Keri Russell

A few months after the announcement of the factory closure...

Bright sunshine streamed through the bedroom window, and as I gazed over the slate rooftops, there wasn't a hint of clouds in the pale blue sky. It was the first warm morning in months and the unexpected heat seemed to give the neighbourhood a boost after a long, drawn-out winter. During breakfast with Fran, a trip to the garden centre was discussed and by late afternoon our patio was once more in bloom, with each terracotta pot filled with colourful flowers.

We also purchased bags of charcoal, in anticipation of many farewell barbeques. Not that we'd done much outdoor cooking before, but now that we'd decided to move to Australia, it felt like the perfect time to practise. Our friends thought we were silly to be spending money on potted plants, considering we'd soon be moving away. But we wanted this spring and summer to feel special, as it might be our last in England for a long time. Maybe forever.

Our first stop would be South America, followed by Africa, and many months later, Australia, to start a new life down under. But before we left, there were so many things we needed to do and so many places we still wanted to explore.

One of these excursions led us to a migration seminar at Sandown Park racecourse, located 20 miles southwest of London. It was during the afternoon interval that our *sliding doors* moment occurred. The presentations were a sell-out, filled with hundreds of Brits in search of a better life in New Zealand or Australia. Migration agents were strategically placed throughout the corridors, handing out giveaways, sweets and stickers, to gain the attention of those passing by.

As we ambled past the stalls, I listened to snippets of conversation between the agents and the hopeful visitors. Time and time again I kept hearing about skills, qualifications, age and experience. In most circumstances, these are the key factors that must be met to gain permanent entry to Australia, based on the number of points you receive in each category. If you tick enough boxes and your skills are in demand, then you could find yourself with enough points to apply for a permanent visa.

Throughout the morning we spoke with a few agents, sat through some slick presentations and then enjoyed a coffee alongside a giant map of Australia, displayed on a wall. We studied the map for a while, alongside other visitors. Some shared with us the places they one day hoped to move to and pointed out towns and cities I knew very little about. They held the last session of the morning in the main auditorium and as we settled into our seats, I stared at the words on the screen:

Come and visit the Sunshine State of Queensland!

A retired couple from South Africa presented the fun-fact slide show. They'd made the move from Durban to the Sunshine Coast and were now on a whirlwind trip to England to share their story. During the interval, we made our way to the nearest café to study the leaflets and flyers we'd collected.

While queuing for coffee, I made eye contact with the man alongside me, and we soon began chatting. Kevin was a short and stocky electrician who'd travelled down from Scunthorpe for the seminar. Without prompting, he began explaining the technicalities of gaining a licence to work as an electrician in Australia. I nodded politely and then studied the colourful cover of a magazine which he'd slid along the counter towards me. A glossy photo, depicting a groomed family of four, took up most of the cover. They seemed to be enjoying a picnic by their caravan, while overlooking a sun-drenched beach.

He edged closer and dropped his voice, as if to spill a secret. 'Take a look inside. It's filled with loads of stories about people who have travelled all over Australia. There's a great article about Adelaide–with photos of all the free barbeques they have in the city. They seem to be everywhere–in parks, by the beach and along the riverfront. Imagine cooking sausages on a free barbeque while enjoying an ocean view, with near guaranteed sunshine. What more could you want?'

'Sounds too good to be true,' I admitted.

He studied me for a moment and then asked, 'Have you applied for a permanent visa yet?'

'No, I'm just here with my wife to learn a little more about Australia and to—'

Without warning, his voice cut across mine. 'I've had enough of England. I hate the traffic jams, grey skies and long winters. I've also had enough of the constant battles between the unions and management and don't even get me started about the state of the economy. The shops are closing down, the...'

While Kevin ranted, I collected my coffee, smiled politely and planned my escape. Just as I stepped away from the counter, he continued again. 'I'm determined to get work in the Australian gold mines. I'm not afraid of a hard day's work and have heard you can earn a fortune. But I've just been chatting to a migration agent about my chances, and she thinks I'll struggle to get a working visa, due to my age.'

Without prompting, he then said, 'I'm 45 next month, which means I might lose a few points towards my application. If you ask me, it's a stupid rule. I'm in my prime, you know. I plan to meet another agent later, as there has to be a way I can get in. I don't mind what I pay, as long as they get me that bit of paper!'

Before I had time to reply, Fran called my name. It was the perfect moment to slip away, so I wished him luck and excused myself. His desperation to move to Australia had unsettled me, as we didn't feel a compelling need to escape forever. We had lots of friends nearby and a caring family that didn't want us to go away for too long.

As for the British weather, we enjoyed the variation that came with four differing seasons. Each winter we'd get away to the snow-clad mountains of Scotland and our summer holidays often involved long weekends on the coast, or treks across parts of the Lake District.

All we were after was the chance to live and work in Australia for a while, so we could take our time to explore the vast country. But as I listened to similar conversations, I sensed that others felt the same as Kevin and wanted to make a real and lasting change to their lives. Australia seemed to be his only goal, but I couldn't help wondering if he was searching for a new life or just running away from a bad one. As I made my way towards Fran, I spotted Kevin again. He was sitting at a nearby table, in deep conversation with another hopeful.

Fran was standing next to a fair-haired couple, both in their early thirties, and I recognised them at once. I'd seen them over the years at various social functions across our hometown, but had rarely spoken to them at length. We soon discovered that Jo and John were visiting the seminar to investigate the best way to run a business in Australia. They'd already been accepted into the country and were now counting down the days. After we'd heard about their plans, John asked, 'So if you get accepted, what part of Australia will you move to?'

This was the first time anyone had ever asked us. Fran and I exchanged looks and grinned sheepishly, as we didn't know the answer. Our prime aim was securing a visa for Australia, but we hadn't thought about which city or region to settle in. Until this point, our thoughts had been about the logistics and emotional strain of such a move. Besides, we were partway through organising a global backpacking adventure. This included the chance to venture into the Amazon jungle, to work as conservation volunteers. The thought of where to live in Australia seemed a long way away.

'Perth is the place!' John exclaimed.

'We love it,' Jo agreed. 'It has a wonderful climate, with guaranteed summers. The beaches are magical, the children have wide open spaces to play in and the lifestyle is laid back, compared with England.'

After multiple visits they knew Australia well, and over another coffee they gave us many reasons why Perth was their pick of all the major cities. For them, this wasn't a travel escapade, but a permanent move to the other side of the world, and it was clear they weren't in a hurry to return.

John's last words as we exchanged email addresses were loud and clear. 'You wait and see, guys. Perth is an amazing place. Make sure you look us up when you get there. We'll look after you!'

And that was our *sliding doors* moment.

I knew nothing about Perth, very little about Australia beyond the brochures, and in a country close to the size of continental USA, only knew four people, all of whom had left my hometown a decade earlier. Now I knew two more who'd soon live there, and according to them, Perth was *the* best place to live in Australia.

During the drive back from the seminar, we chatted excitedly about what lay ahead. Would we choose Perth to live in or try our luck in Queensland, just like the retired couple from South Africa? Tasmania sounded appealing, but a little too breezy for my liking. The *Top End* of the Northern Territory sounded extreme in every way, with six differing seasons according to the Aboriginal communities that live close by. During the year, the vast plains experience monsoonal flooding followed by long periods of sunshine and sweltering daytime temperatures. It is here that you will find crocodile infested rivers, majestic waterfalls, steep gorges and very few people!

With a spring in our step, we arrived back home and set about making plans for our overseas adventure. As the summer months flew past, we sent out invites to friends and family to enjoy a barbeque together, but the weather always seemed to take a turn for the worse each weekend.

By the end of August, I was out of a job, along with many other workers. The factory gates had finally closed and with just one weekend left before the end of summer, the only task remaining was to enjoy a barbeque. I ventured into the back garden, gazed up at the black clouds brooding overhead, and searched for gaps between them. Any hint of blue, no matter how small, meant hope. I pulled the portable barbeque out of the garden shed, gave it a clean and went shopping for sausages.

Before leaving the supermarket, I grabbed a six-pack of Australian beer and stashed it alongside the meat and salad. I'd once heard that Australians purchase beer without leaving their cars, with drive-through bottle shops a common sight across the country. That kind of shopping trip was all in the future. What mattered right now was getting the barbeque underway.

During the previous months, I'd read so much about Australia and its people, in various blog posts and online forums, that I no longer knew fact from fiction. Did the citizens of Australia really enjoy barbeques each weekend? Compared with my once-a-year effort, it seemed a lot. Would I have to check under the toilet seats while in Sydney, in case I found the deadly funnel-web spider?

I still had no idea what the Australian national game was. Most websites insisted it was cricket, others declared it to be horse racing, and other forums swore it was football. Further investigation revealed that their brand of football is a far cry from the world game played by teams such as Manchester United, Liverpool and Barcelona. Instead, they use an oval-shaped football and teams can even score a point when they miss the main goal. It was clear that I had a lot to learn.

The last few weeks had been emotional, with the growing realisation that our life in England was coming to a close. Somewhere, shrouded in the unknown and far away, lay a new life in a foreign land. Each morning I'd wake with a jolt, instantly aware that our departure was a day nearer, and would spend the day flushed with excitement.

Each evening the demons stalked my thoughts, as I battled with the notion of leaving my dad behind. Luckily, there were other siblings living nearby, but that still didn't stop the guilt. I knew he would adore the sunshine whenever he visited, but somehow this didn't seem to justify our need to move half a world away.

During the drive home from the shops, I detoured towards my childhood suburb and took a walk down memory lane. I'd once known every family in the street, and over the years we'd become a happy, bustling community. Back doors were rarely locked, children played outside all day and happily constructed custom bikes from various parts given freely by neighbours. It was the type of street where you knocked on doors when you'd run out of sugar or needed to borrow something. I grew up calling the closest neighbours 'Uncle' or 'Auntie,' even though we weren't related. At the time, it had seemed so natural.

I stood outside the house where I'd been raised and caught the faint smell of exotic spices in the cool breeze, as the residents prepared their evening meal. I wanted to knock on the familiar door, hoping to be invited in for an impromptu tour, but it wouldn't be the same. Not anymore. This was their home now, and my childhood was over. It was time to move on.

I turned away and studied the street sign before gazing at the familiar surroundings. Littlefield Road hadn't changed much over the years. Some homes looked slightly worn and in need of a makeover, but most seemed well cared for, with flowerbeds along the edges of the front lawns adding a touch of colour to the dreary day.

The houses faced an oval expanse of grass, which many in our street had known as *The Green*. Throughout my childhood, it became the setting for friendly kicks of the ball, to prepare for epic football matches against the kids from the next estate.

Since then, a handful of trees had been planted close to the perimeter by the local council, including a few that looked ridiculously close to where corner kicks would once have been taken. Parking bays had also been cut into the edges, further diminishing the grassy footprint. The remaining space still looked large enough for a decent game of football, but there was no sign of any children to confirm this.

I strolled into the middle of the oval, closed my eyes and thought back to those long summer days, when games had lasted for hours. Over the years there had been fiery tackles, the odd tantrum, dazzling skills worthy of a scout's eye, heaps of goals and plenty of laughter. By late afternoon, the games fizzled out, with each player reluctantly picking a jumper from the pile and heading home after the last call from their mum.

The sound of a barking dog shook me from the daydream. A large Alsatian bounded past my legs, away from its owner, a wiry teenager weighed down by a puffer jacket. While walking past he dropped his eyes and ignored the dog, which was sniffing the ground in preparation for doing its business. The teenager strolled across the oval without a backward glance.

Did he know that his dog was dropping a turd on my childhood football pitch? By the time I contemplated calling him back, he'd reached the edge of the oval, with the dog in pursuit.

It was also time for me to make haste. My days of navigating the narrow roads near the town centre were coming to an end. Within a month we'd be working as conservation volunteers in the Amazon jungle, and a year from now I hoped to be driving along remote outback roads, under endless blue skies.

As expected, my street was jammed on both sides with parked cars, lined bumper to bumper, which forced me up the hill in search of a vacant space. Maybe our future house in Australia would have a driveway with a garage and a place to store surfboards. The thought of living near the ocean prompted a hearty chuckle, and I found myself humming a tune as I opened the front door.

Our little piece of England was hemmed in on all sides by century-old houses. With no high fences between the narrow back gardens, privacy was a rare event. Initially, I'd enjoyed standing in our garden while chatting about the weather with neighbours five houses away, but after a few summers the novelty had grown thin.

The chance of rain seemed to have chased the neighbourhood gardeners inside, and for once I found myself alone as I crossed the lawn towards the shed, in search of charcoal. After positioning the barbeque on my patio, I tipped a generous handful of coals into the belly and doused them in lighter fuel.

There was no sign of blue in the sky anymore, but I felt committed to continue and decided it was time for music and refreshments. As I cracked open a can of Victoria Bitter, I heard the familiar shuffle of slippers on concrete and looked up expectantly. My next-door neighbour had come outside to investigate.

John was long into retirement. He'd served in the army for many years, before transferring to the post office, until they bade him farewell with a pension and a gold watch. He was short and stocky and blessed with a trimmed thatch of grey hair. Now over eighty, his faculties were still intact, and his inquisitive eyes rarely missed anything new that had been added to our patio.

He let me prepare my music collection, and as the familiar sound of Brit Pop pulsated from the speakers, he ambled closer and rested his arms across the mesh fence that divided our gardens. 'What's that racket you're playing, Alistair?'

'They're a band called Oasis, John. It's the kind of music you play during the last weekend of summer. You know, to get you in the mood for a barbeque.'

He stared past me, his eyes on the speakers. 'Sorry, but I can't hear what you're saying with all that noise.'

I turned the volume down, so it now resembled background music in a department store. 'How's that, John?'

'Much better.'

Then he pointed to the barbeque and asked, 'What's that for?'

I knew he was aware. It was a game we played every time something new appeared in our garden. My decision to paint our garden shed in a shade of duck-egg blue, still bemused him. Time and time again he'd come out to investigate, as I splashed paint across the weathered timbers, to transform the shed into something that resembled a beach hut.

'Sheds aren't meant to be blue. They're always brown. It looks daft if you ask me.'

While standing halfway up the stepladder, I'd smile and wave back. 'I've got some spare paint if you need it, John. I'll come over later if you want, to help spruce up yours. Colourful sheds are all the rage, you know!'

'Not on your nelly, mate,' he'd reply, before heading inside for his afternoon cuppa.

The incident had occurred the previous summer and was still a topic he liked to raise. Although I enjoyed our chats over the fence, it was clear we were poles apart. Over the years, he'd witnessed a lot of changes in the neighbourhood. Some of the largest houses had been converted into flats, which meant more cars, more people and fewer families.

John would never move away and often reminisced about the past. I was looking only to the future and had grown weary of the street. There was nowhere to park, each new neighbour seemed less friendly than the last and the back gardens were barely wide enough to swing a cricket bat.

My latest neighbours on the other side had recently arrived from Zimbabwe. At first, they seemed friendly enough and knocks on the door to ask for sugar or tea seemed quaint. That's what neighbours have always done, and we gave happily, including a few occasions when we'd invited them in for tea and cake. During one such visit, they informed us they were economic refugees, forced out of the country because of tribal unrest. At first, I thought they were a family of five, but during the last few months, their numbers had grown.

I no longer had any idea how many people lived in their three-bedroom terrace, but their front door seemed to be forever opening and closing throughout night and day. Just lately, the stench coming from their overgrown garden was in danger of souring international relations. I also sensed a sugar embargo coming on, unless they removed the worn mattress and broken settee from the shared alleyway.

John pulled me from my daydream as he pointed to the sky and said, 'Have you seen those clouds? There's rain on the way. I hope you've got an umbrella.'

I dismissed his remarks with a nonchalant shrug, but deep down, sensed disaster. Reaching for my beer, I peered towards the skyline. The only blue I could see now was my garden shed, and apart from the green grass, every other colour looked grey and depressing. I turned my attention back to John and asked, 'Do you fancy a sausage later? They're special ones, with pork and herbs.'

He studied the gathering clouds and replied, 'Why don't you just grill them in the kitchen, like normal people?'

'I'm practising for Australia, John. Apparently, you have to prove to the government that you can barbeque effectively. Otherwise they won't let you in the country.'

He ignored my stab at humour and watched as match after match failed to light the coals. Although he knew we were moving to Australia, it was a topic he rarely mentioned, except to remind me it was far away, stinking hot and inhabited by man-eating crocodiles!

While he watched my every move, I forced a smile and lit another match. Just then, the wind dropped, and I heard a whooshing sound, followed by a sharp crackle as the fuel ignited, sending a hazy fireball into the air. In celebration, I raised my beer and turned to face John. He shook his head and said, 'Well, that took ages, didn't it?'

I felt too elated to reply and raced inside for the sausages, along with a woollen jumper and an umbrella. By the time I returned, John was nowhere in sight.

Fran arrived at teatime, clutching a chilled bottle of chardonnay. Together, we sat in the fading light, determined to experience at least one outdoor meal before summer ended. Protected by our umbrella, we ignored the drizzle falling from the granite skies and concentrated instead on enjoying the sausages, while going over the last details of our overseas adventure.

We'd miss John, with his curious nature and wry humour. His petite wife, Wynn, had always been generous, with homemade cakes on offer whenever we popped around for afternoon tea. But those days were soon to be over, and our house was about to be rented out. We'd already started packing our essentials into cardboard boxes, in readiness for their transportation to Australia. Tomorrow we'd go shopping for rucksacks, sleeping bags and walking boots. As we finished the last of the summer wine, I gazed over the grey roofline, dreaming of cooking barbeques Down Under, while dressed in a singlet and shorts.

The Indian summer arrived just in time for our day of departure. While walking towards the garden shed to double-check the lock, I heard the pleasant sound of children's laughter. A newly arrived family that lived three houses away were enjoying the autumn sunshine, with squeals from the toddlers as they trundled along the paving on their scooters, while their mum pegged washing on the line.

Her husband was watering a flowerbed, turning the hosepipe towards his giggling children as they raced past. He noticed me watching and waved. When they'd first moved in, we'd exchanged names from afar, but were yet to catch up. He was pointing to the cloudless sky and saying something, but the children's laughter drowned out his words. I felt like replying, *I'm sorry for not getting to know you more, but we're off to Australia to learn how to surf.*

I realised how strange this would sound and instead called out, 'What amazing weather! Anyone would think we're living in Australia.'

A wailing child distracted him, and as he knelt to investigate, I walked back inside, just as there was a knock on the front door. It was Fran's mum and dad, which signalled that our departure was imminent.

To enjoy the midday sunshine, two young men from next door had dragged their discarded settee from the alleyway and placed it on the pavement. They wore Arsenal football shirts and were sprawled across the matted seats, watching cars and buses pass by. As we emerged from the house for the last time, they raised their beer cans and wished us good luck, then giggled softly as we struggled to cram our luggage into the car.

John and Wynn opened their front door to bid us farewell, but never ventured onto the street. Suddenly, it was all too real. Tears welled in Fran's eyes and she rushed towards them, gripping my hand as I ran alongside her. For a few precious seconds we hugged them closely, then shook their hands and promised to stay in touch.

As we drove away from the kerbside, I watched John and Wynn, waving from their doorway. From the back seat, I raised my hand in a farewell gesture but deep down felt a stab of guilt, as if we were abandoning them. I hoped they had plenty of sugar and tea in the pantry, as they could expect a knock on the door any time soon.

Strangers in the Night

"In the end, we only regret the chances we didn't take."
– Lewis Carroll

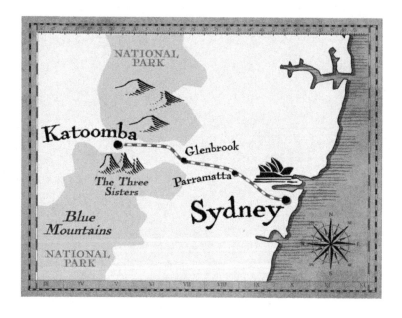

After waving farewell to John and Wynn, we set off on our round-the-world adventure. Along the way, we worked as conservation volunteers in the jungles of Ecuador and signed up for Spanish school to learn the language. In the Andes of Peru, we hired donkeys and a guide to tackle a remote mountain pass. Later, we trekked along the Inca Trail, before heading overland to Bolivia to explore the high-altitude plateau. Near the edge of a mining village, we stumbled upon the remains of Butch Cassidy and the Sundance Kid, two of the most famous outlaws from the Wild West. Days later, we were deep underground in a silver mine, running for our lives from an explosion!

From South America, we headed to Africa for the chance to climb Kilimanjaro and explore the island of Zanzibar. We then signed up as passengers for an overland trucking adventure, which took us through Botswana, Namibia and South Africa, camping in the wilds and listening to lions as they prowled nearby. We also survived a white-knuckle rafting trip on the Zambezi, tackling grade-five rapids with the help of an experienced guide. Finally, we made our way to Cape Town, to set eyes upon the prison bars that once held Nelson Mandela.

During our travels, Fran continually kept in contact with Jo and John, the couple we'd met at the migration seminar. They were now living their dream, after moving to the west coast of Australia. Our plan was to fly from Johannesburg to Sydney and visit some of the places where Fran had once lived and worked. A few weeks before our flight, she discovered that there was a technical issue with her application to live and work in Australia.

Years before, she'd worked in Romania for an international charity that specialised in supporting orphanages. The Australian Government needed a police clearance from the Romanian authorities, before her application could continue. Despite many calls to the charity and the Romanian police department, Fran couldn't get the information she needed. She decided that the only way to ensure a speedy outcome was to fly to Romania and travel to the town where she'd once lived and worked.

There were tears at Johannesburg airport as we prepared to go our separate ways. I had the better deal, as my flight was heading towards an Australian summer. Fran was taking a long-haul flight towards a Romanian winter. As we sat in a café while waiting to board, Fran sipped her coffee and said, 'Don't forget to get in touch with Jo and John when you touch down, to let them know you're finally in Australia.'

I didn't have the heart to tell her they'd be on the west coast, thousands of kilometres away, in Perth. They may as well have been in a different country. She was showing signs of distress at the thought of missing out on the chance to travel to Sydney with me.

I still remember her parting words before she headed towards her departure gate. 'I can't believe I'm not going with you. Please try out a few nights in Glebe. When I backpacked around Australia years ago, it was my favourite part of Sydney and I'd love to hear what it's like these days.'

Sydney came with high expectations, but damp weather and thoughts of Fran in transit cooled my enthusiasm as the plane touched down after the overnight flight. In the airport arrivals lounge, I discovered a wall filled with colourful advertisements for budget hotels and youth hostels. After a quick search I found the hostel that Fran had recommended, but as I picked up the complimentary phone, a glimmer of doubt crossed my mind.

Over the years, I've learned through trial and error, that I no longer think of hostel dormitories as a frugal way to meet interesting travellers from across the world. I've been caught out too many times by friendly backpackers, who display perfect manners in the communal kitchen, but turn out to have strange habits once they head to bed.

There are those who can wake the dead with their snores, others who toss and turn between coughing bouts, and more than a few who rise at dawn, rustling through bags in search of clothes before heading to the communal shower. Although I yearned for a few nights of comfort, I couldn't ignore the dent in our budget, because of Fran's unplanned visit to Romania.

With a shrug of the shoulders, I punched in the hostel's number, hoping the dormitories would be full and that a single room with a power shower would be the only option available. The call was answered briskly, although the female accent on the other end of the phone sounded Nordic rather than Australian. 'Good morning, this is Glebe Backpackers. How can I help?'

'Hi there, I've just landed in Sydney and am after a bed for three nights. Do you have any vacancies, please?'

'I'm afraid our single rooms are all taken. Your only option is a dormitory, and you're in luck as I have one bed left, in a room of four. Have you stayed here before?'

'No, but my wife has, about 15 years ago. She's out of the country at the moment but was keen for me to try your hostel. I guess it's changed over the years.'

'I wouldn't know what it was like back then, but it's very popular nowadays, especially with students taking time out. Are you doing something similar?'

'No, I'm afraid not. My gap year days are well and truly over. I'm nearer 40 than 30 but am not over the hill just yet.'

'That's good, as we like the young at heart. Do you want me to book you in then?'

As she spoke, my eyes were drawn to the long list of other hostels. No doubt some would have single rooms, but I'd already promised Fran that I'd give this one a go. Reluctantly, I answered yes and gave her my name.

'That's great, Alistair. The shuttle bus leaves every 30 minutes from outside the terminal. See you soon.'

The line went dead, so I picked up my rucksack and made my way to the exit. As the automatic doors opened wide, I stepped onto the pavement and stood for a few moments in the sunshine, smiling widely. I'd finally made it to Australia, after so many years. Although it seemed strange to be here without Fran, I knew she'd want me to enjoy every moment. With this thought in my mind, I strode purposely towards the shuttle bus, just across the road.

The route took us through the heart of the city, but after watching folks go about their everyday life, it dawned on me how ordinary they seemed. I'd imagined that most citizens would be tanned, but those on their way to work looked pasty and in need of a holiday.

Instead of Sydney, I could have been in London on a spring day. Even the passing clouds resembled those I'd often seen in England. The cars that idled at the traffic lights were comparable to those I'd seen in Europe, and many pedestrians looked as if they would rather be somewhere else. Some drank coffee from takeaway cups, others spoke into phones, and one or two raised their eyes to the darkening sky while they waited to cross the intersections.

The bus dropped me in Glebe and I entered the hostel with a bright demeanour, determined to enjoy my time in Sydney. A curvaceous woman with long blonde hair and honey-brown eyes was sitting behind the front desk. She welcomed me with a Hollywood smile and said, 'Good morning. I'm guessing you go by the name of Alistair.'

I smiled in acknowledgement and planted my rucksack on the floor. From a nearby room, I heard laughter and the sound of a plastic ball being hit by bats. Two men walked past, both holding bottles of beer, which they swigged down in gulps. They looked at least 15 years my junior, and for the first time since leaving England, I felt out of place.

I contemplated making a swift U-turn, but the receptionist had already seduced the credit card from my wallet. As she completed the transaction, a raucous group of lads crashed through the main entrance, singing pop songs while on their way to the outside pool. She handed back my card and said, 'It looks like they don't want the party to end. But don't worry, as I think there's a storm on the way. With luck, they'll be asleep soon. Come on–I'll show you to your room.'

My dormitory was at the end of a long corridor, and as she opened the door a waft of stale air greeted us. I stepped inside and studied the cramped room. A dirty plate took centre stage in the middle of the vinyl floor, with remnants of a recent take-away smeared across the edges.

I stepped over a discarded pair of jeans and made a note of the antique chair by the solitary window. Its velvet-lined cushion looked inviting but was now home to a crumpled pair of boxer shorts. Apart from the bunk beds, the only other furniture was a narrow sink, an adjacent mirror and a wooden table littered with an assortment of shaving foams, deodorants, after-shaves and toothpastes.

I soon discovered that my roommates were three nocturnal Norwegians who arrived home in the early hours in a blaze of noise, farts and drunken laughter. During the first morning, I hid under the thin sheets, while they retold drinking stories to each other and staggered around the room.

I ventured out on the town with them the following evening, but it soon became clear that we were on different journeys. They were out for maximum alcohol intake, with minimum expenditure. I was looking for the chance to soak up the culture, while trying a few locally crafted beers and listening to live music.

To escape from the Norwegians, I tried my luck in the city centre instead. The modern hostel that I picked lacked the retro feel of the Glebe establishment, but at least the stylish décor and firmer bed offered the chance of greater comfort. I still couldn't find a single room and was now in a dormitory with a group of three crisp-crunching nerds from Northampton, England.

They'd initially greeted me with lukewarm smiles, as they sat side by side on a top bunk, before returning their attention to mobile phones and laptops. A large bottle of Coke sat un-opened at the end of one bed, along with a few empty packets of chocolate. While they munched together on a family-sized packet of salt and vinegar crisps, I shared my name and waited for them to do the same.

Between mouthfuls, they gave their names as Daniel, Benjamin and Thomas. Further investigation revealed that they were partway through a gap year from university, while study-ing for degrees in computer science.

During the next few hours I went out for provisions, took a stroll around the block to get my bearings and spent time in a second-hand bookshop, browsing for something to enjoy while lazing on Bondi Beach. I then cooked up a simple noodle dish in the communal kitchen, washed down with an ice-cold beer.

On my return to the room, the three young men were still on the same bunk bed. Despite their youth, they looked far too pasty, with bloodshot eyes that refused to pry away from the technology in their hands.

The Coke bottle was empty, and they were now partway through a family-sized packet of cheese and onion crisps. With nightfall approaching, I felt the need to get out of the hostel and into the city. While I sorted through my clothes, Benjamin made a dash for the doorway and returned a few minutes later, holding three large pizzas.

While he clambered up the ladder towards his mates, I asked how they were enjoying their time in Sydney. Daniel and Thomas simultaneously turned to face Benjamin, who was the spokesman of the nerdy trio.

While his friends tucked into pepperoni slices, Benjamin smiled down at me from the top bunk and said, 'It's okay, I guess. I haven't seen that much to be truthful, apart from the opera house on the day we arrived.'

'So, what do you do each day?' I asked.

'We just hang out and play games. We might head out for another pizza later, to the place up the road that just delivered these. You should try them out sometime.'

I decided it was time to ask the obvious question. 'Couldn't you just do that kind of thing back in England?'

'Yes, but it's much warmer here.'

'But you don't seem to get out much. Apart from going out for pizzas, have you explored any of the city?'

'I went to the shops yesterday, for new batteries.'

'How far away was that?'

'Just across the road?'

I needed to change my line of questioning to unravel why they'd travelled all the way from England to sit for hours on a top bunk in a Sydney youth hostel!

'Where are you heading to, after here? Are you planning a road trip anywhere?'

Benjamin glanced at his two mates, but there was no response. Once again, their focus had been stolen by technology, regardless of the conversation going on around them. His answer was whisper quiet. 'I'm not sure, really. We've got six months in Australia and are just taking our time.'

And with that, he wolfed down a slice of pizza, picked up his phone and started tapping. I left them alone and tried chatting again the following evening. As before, they sat together on the top bunk, glued to technology, while enjoying crisps.

I hadn't heard from Fran in days, but instead of rejoicing in the fact that I had Sydney to myself, I traipsed around the city in search of someone to talk to. Once or twice I tried making conversation with other travellers but couldn't seem to make a connection. My day trip to Bondi fared better, including the chance to play beach volleyball with a group of South American backpackers.

Squally showers cut the game short, and I soon learned they were on the move from Sydney, heading north, with Byron Bay on their mind. As the cold front continued, I spent the days wandering between museums, coffee shops and pubs. Each time I returned to my room, the dynamic trio were still there, either drinking Coke, munching on crisps or playing games on their gadgets.

A showdown was imminent, and it came unexpectedly in the early hours of the third night. I'd returned from an evening at an Irish bar, eager for sleep after a few pints of Guinness. They were still awake and after exchanging pleasantries I bade them goodnight and clambered onto my top bunk. With ear plugs inserted and a blanket to cover my body, the Guinness took over and I soon drifted to sleep.

Hours later, I woke with a start and checked the time. It was three in the morning, and although the light was off, a soft glow radiated from across the room. One of my earplugs had fallen out, and the blanket lay bedraggled near my feet. I could hear the rustle of plastic bags and the crunching of biscuits, so I sat up, rubbed my eyes and stared across the room. Despite the darkness, I could make out their silhouettes, sitting together on the opposite bunk, playing games on their phones. I then heard a beep from an incoming message, followed by high-pitched laughter.

'That's it!' I yelled into the dark. 'For the last three nights you've laid in bed, texting your geeky mates back at home, or playing video games while munching on crisps and doughnuts. You've got 15 seconds to turn off all electronic devices, move all plastic bags out of reach, and finish any food. If I hear one more rustle of plastic or the beeping of a phone between now and the morning, I'll throw all electronic devices out of the window.'

Surprisingly, they didn't say a word, or attack me with pillows after I'd gone back to sleep. By the time I stirred, they'd cleared out of the room, leaving a trail of empty crisp packets in their wake. I could have waited to see who my next roommates would be but decided to get out of the city. Despite the iconic attractions and manicured parks, Sydney was proving to be far less appealing without my wife. It was time for a change of scenery.

The Blue Mountains National Park is estimated to be 50 million years old, with a footprint that spans over 2,500 square kilometres. It is situated 90 kilometres west of Sydney and is famed for its vast tracts of eucalyptus forests, deep gorges and fast-flowing rivers. It is also renowned for its contribution to conservation and has gained status as a UNESCO World Heritage Site. If ever there was a location where I could escape from the crisp-crunching nerds, this was the place.

The national park gets its name from the fine blueish haze that blankets the region when viewed from a distance. The hills, valleys and escarpments are home to many species of eucalyptus and gum trees, all of which disperse tiny droplets of oil from their leaves into the atmosphere. Whenever these oils combine with water vapour and early sunlight, the blueish haze appears.

I travelled by train, and during the two-hour journey watched as the city gave way to bushland. It wasn't only the houses and factory units that dwindled from sight, but also the clouds, which faded from view with every gentle curve of the track.

My destination was the town of Katoomba, the largest settlement within the national park. As soon as I disembarked, the lethargy and loneliness that I'd felt in Sydney ebbed away, replaced by a surge of enthusiasm. The town had the look and feel of a quirky backwater, but also the vibrancy and intimacy of a place where nature lovers coexist alongside artisans, musicians and the sporty. Trekkers meandered along the café-lined high street, mingling with window shoppers and photographers, in a scene reminiscent of the Lake District in England.

The youth hostel I chose had been tastefully restored to reflect its art déco history and even had an available single room, complete with a powerful shower. During the next few days I ventured into the nearby hills, walking for hours along narrow trails and steep paths. Sometimes I'd encounter groups of walkers at lookout points or at the base of waterfalls. But within a few strides, I'd be alone once more, surrounded by majestic gum trees as I headed to the next destination on my map.

I also trekked towards the Three Sisters, a triple-peaked sandstone formation over 900 metres high, which towers over Jamison Valley. From up high, I had commanding views of the surrounding forest, broken in places by steep cliffs and rivers. The fresh air and stunning scenery reinvigorated my appetite for conversation. Each evening, while cooking simple pasta dishes, I nattered away to travellers from across the world. On one occasion, while searching for chilli flakes in the pantry, I discovered a sign by the door.

Please don't leave the Blue Mountains without experiencing canyoning. It's like leaving Las Vegas without enjoying a show.

After reading the sign, I made my way to the hostel receptionist and booked a spot for the following day. She then handed over a slip of paper and asked me to wait by the roadside in the morning. All I needed to bring was a change of clothing, a towel, a packed lunch and a water bottle.

I woke to blue skies and treated myself to a cooked breakfast, in readiness for a day of adventure. As instructed, I arrived at the agreed meeting spot just before ten, but found myself alone outside the hostel. Within moments, I was joined by an excited group of tourists, all carrying small backpacks, and dressed in T-shirts, shorts and training shoes. They looked to be in their late teens and as they huddled nearby one of them called out to me. 'Good morning. You are the guide, yes?'

The young man asking had a mop of dark hair and a jolly face. Before I could answer, he stepped closer and said, 'My name is Kaioti, but my English is not so good.'

'I'm Alistair, and your English sounds great. But I'm not your guide and have signed up for canyoning, just like you.'

He nodded politely and gestured towards his friends. I soon learned they were studying in Sydney, after arriving from Japan a few months earlier. The trip to the Blue Mountains was their first foray out of the city, to celebrate the end of the semester. I smiled in acknowledgement and turned my attention to one of the girls. 'Are you excited about going canyoning?'

She glanced towards Kaioti with quizzical eyes and waited for him to translate my question. In response, she called out something in Japanese, which resulted in a ripple of laughter from the other students. Kaioti then translated her answer back into English for me. 'She excited–yes, but a little scared. You know, because of the danger–with snakes and spiders.'

Out of the corner of my eye, I then caught sight of another man, standing head and shoulders above the students. He had cropped blonde hair, wide shoulders and sharp blue eyes. In a booming voice, he called out, 'Don't worry about the snakes, as they normally keep out of your way unless they feel threatened.'

Kaioti turned towards him and said, 'Ah, that is very good to know, thank you.' He then nodded slightly and asked, 'Are you our guide?'

The man smiled brightly and shook his head. 'No, I am Walter, from Germany. I am booked on the tour, the same as you.'

By now, all eyes were on the street, for anyone that resembled a tour guide. While we waited, I started chatting with Walter. His clipped voice carried far as he explained the events that had led him from Germany to Australia. 'I'm taking a break from university, to visit some of my family that live overseas. I have an auntie in Sydney and decided to take a trip to the Blue Mountains. My hometown is close to the German Alps, so I am used to spending time in the mountains, but since arriving in Katoomba, all I have seen are a few hills and lots of trees.'

Walter continued to chat away, seemingly oblivious to some of the Japanese, who'd slowly retreated to the hostel doorway. I stayed put, along with Kaioti, as Walter rattled through the various countries on his wish list. Eventually, Kaioti made his excuses and returned to his friends. I stayed put, nodding and smiling, while waiting for Walter to take a breath.

On hearing about his cousin who worked as a doctor in Tanzania, I found the perfect opportunity to get a word in. 'Oh, you'll love Tanzania. I went there last year to climb Kilimanjaro with—'

He cut in with a swift reply. 'Did you know that very few people actually *climb* Kilimanjaro? Most of them *trek* to the top, through rainforest and tundra, before heading towards the glacier. My cousin thinks I should climb Mount Kenya instead, as it's far more challenging. I love winter sports and was captain of my university skiing team last year.'

There was no way I could compete with Walter's sporting exploits, so I should have walked away or changed conversation. Instead, I played my best card. 'I enjoy visiting the Alps as well and once climbed to the summit of Mont Blanc, with two friends. It's the highest—'

'Which route did you take?'

His question took me by surprise, and I couldn't remember the exact answer. In reply, I said, 'I think we stayed overnight in the Goûter Hut, before—'

Walter cut in once again, smiling in acknowledgement. 'That's how most climbers go, especially those with less mountaineering experience. I climbed to the top last summer, using the Cosmique Route. I was after a technical challenge with fewer climbers around.'

By now, I could feel the heat rising to my cheeks. The climb to the top of Mont Blanc had been one of the hardest challenges of my life. At 4,810 metres, it's the highest peak in Western Europe, and although tame compared to the multitude of sheer-sided mountains nearby, is still a formidable test for any newcomer to the Alps. I'd used ice axes at one point and had even lost my footing in a crevasse while trudging through knee-deep snow. Together with two friends and a guide, we'd reached the frozen summit in time for a magical sunrise, after leaving the overnight hut five hours earlier.

Now I was standing next to Walter, who seemed almost superhuman compared to me. While I planned my escape, he started up again. 'I hear we will go abseiling today. Have you tried it before?'

His question gave me the perfect reason to smile. I gathered my thoughts and said, 'Now that you mention it, I once—'

Walter didn't wait for me to finish. Instead, he began explaining about the indoor climbing wall he visited most weekends, when back at home. Instead of listening any longer, I contemplated a dash to the nearest café for a takeaway coffee.

With perfect timing, two men arrived on the scene. One had a climbing rope coiled over a shoulder and the other had a large rucksack strapped to his back. Kaioti stepped away from his friends and asked the inevitable question. 'Good morning. Are you our guides?'

Heath and Peter were both tall and gangly, with welcoming smiles and firm handshakes. They looked to be in their mid-twenties, with shoulder-length hair and sun-kissed faces. After brief introductions, they led us around the corner, towards a parked minivan.

Just before we drove off, Peter held up several pieces of paper and called for our attention. 'I'm looking forward to showing you some special places today. At times, we'll encounter rock pools, waterfalls and narrow tracks through the forest. I've got wetsuits and harnesses to hand out later, which will help keep you warm and protected. With this in mind, I need each of you to sign a disclosure form. The small print mentions that if you slip, fall, get bitten by a snake, break a leg, get crushed by a falling rock, or attacked by a drop bear, it's all your fault, not mine!'

He then smiled and winked before calling out, 'Please don't look so worried. I've been doing this for nearly three years and haven't lost anybody yet. It's rare to see bears dropping from trees around these parts, so if you spot one during our travels, please let me know.'

And with that, we cheerfully signed our lives away and sat back to prepare for the short drive to the starting point. During the journey, Kaioti leaned towards me, his expression deadpan. 'Excuse me, please. Did he say that bears drop from trees? Are they big?'

I smiled and said, 'He mentioned bears, but don't worry as there's no such thing as a drop bear. It's just a joke they play on tourists like you and me. The only bears in the wilds of Australia are koalas, and as far as I know, they are cute and cuddly and don't drop on anyone.'

He relaxed before sharing the good news with his friends. Twenty minutes later, we emerged from the bus into bright sunlight. The first thing I noticed was the sweet smell of eucalyptus that hung in the air. I breathed in deeply, convinced that I could taste honey and menthol at the back of my throat.

Birds darted from tree to tree and insects droned past, as we stood in a semicircle listening to a safety briefing by Heath. He then took a guess at our heights and weights before handing out wetsuits, harnesses and helmets. After wriggling into my wetsuit, I helped some of the students, who tugged at their zips while in fits of giggles.

Whether they were nervous or happy, I wasn't sure, but there was little time to find out as Heath was calling for us to get moving. He then led us through a tree-lined gap, towards the sound of running water. With each step along a narrow trail, the surrounding trees dwindled in size, as we entered a shadowy world, filled with giant boulders that dwarfed those walking alongside. As the temperature dropped, we followed an ancient watercourse, formed over millions of years.

Occasionally, we encountered sparkling streams, all of which fed into ours. Soon we were wading through waist-deep water, its temperature so cold that each of us gasped as we momentarily ducked below the surface. As the trapped water between my skin and the wetsuit warmed, I stopped to study the surroundings. Far above, I noticed a glint of sunlight striking the top of distant pinnacles.

The turbulent water had carved some rocks into half pipes, and it was here that we learned to trust in our guides. Peter went first and positioned himself in a semicircular ingress, which angled downhill towards a pool of clear water. As soon as he let go of the sides, the lively stream of water under his bottom propelled him towards the plunge pool. After surfacing, he urged us to follow, one by one.

Walter followed suit and laid flat on his back, as though he was on a luge in the Winter Olympics. He pushed off without a word and sped down the slippery incline towards the water. Kaioti volunteered next and let out a joyful squeal during his short, but exhilarating journey.

For the next few hours, we traversed many gorges, seeking opportunities to leap into deep pools or scramble up rocky inclines towards the sunshine. Each new encounter seemed to lift the spirits of the Japanese, who often wanted to stop to take photos. Later, we waded through knee-deep pools, with the walls of the canyon so close that we could touch both sides. Along the way, the guides shared the history of the Blue Mountains and explained their ecological importance.

They also pointed out yabbies, sheltering in rock pools, and described how delicious the freshwater crustaceans tasted when grilled on a barbeque. But the only things we would take from the gorges were memories and photographs. After a late snack near the edge of a waterfall, Peter declared that the trip was nearly over, with one more obstacle to overcome.

In response, Walter called out, 'I don't understand. I thought we'd be out until sunset. So far, I have hardly raised a sweat. The receptionist at the hostel told me it would be a challenging excursion, but—'

It was Heath who answered first. 'Walter, you seem like a man of many talents, so maybe you should book the advanced trip for tomorrow. Anyway, by the time we complete the abseil and then hike back to the top, the day will be ending. In Australia, we call that beer o'clock!'

He then winked at the students, before pointing towards a narrow but feisty river, which fell away at an overhang. 'Walter, as you can see, there's one more hurdle for us all. Hopefully, this one will live up to your expectations. The river drops off and turns into a 30-metre waterfall. Our last challenge is to abseil down it, towards the forest floor.'

In reply, Walter shrugged his shoulders. 'Thirty metres is nothing. I can probably abseil down with four or five kicks from the rock face.'

Instead of listening to Walter, I went in search of Peter and led him to one side. 'Is it possible to abseil to the bottom in one go without touching the sides, as I'd like to beat Walter at something today?'

Peter shook his head and smiled. 'No way, mate. The aim here is just to have some fun, not to compete.'

After making his point known, he then offered some advice. 'The falls are vertical at the start, but just after the halfway point you'll come to an angled slab of rock, so you'll need to do lots of bunny hops. The best tip I can give you is to push off hard from the top and let the figure-of-eight do all the work. One thing for sure, you're about to get soaked!'

While waiting for the guides to prepare the ropes, I went in search of a photo opportunity. Just off the track I found a shaded glen, filled with vibrant ferns and a bubbling stream, which seemed to trickle up from the ground before finding a channel between moss-covered boulders.

By the time I returned, Peter was standing by the edge of the gulley, secured by a rope. 'Listen up, everyone. Heath is in position at the base of the waterfall. If you lose control while abseiling, he'll pull on the safety rope to stop you.'

He then called us forward, one by one, to be connected to the main rope. I opted to go last and watched from a safe distance as they lowered each participant over the precipice. Walter went first, and as expected, needed little help. He calmly waved to those left behind, before stepping backwards over the ledge. Kaioti followed soon after, inching his way towards the point of no return, while being coaxed by Peter.

When my turn came, I felt determined to mimic Walter's vigour and kicked off from the top. All at once, I found myself at the mercy of the rushing water, pounding my head and upper body. I couldn't look up because of the force of the water, so tried looking down to see how far I had to go. After blinking away the spray, I could just make out the shape of a man, far below, surrounded by greenery.

I steadied my feet against the buttress and kicked off again, but didn't get far, as I'd come to the angled slab of rock. The water cascaded across the smooth face in a silky sheen, which made it near impossible for my feet to gain traction. After a few bunny hops, my feet landed on a craggy overhang which stopped me in my tracks.

Just before pushing off, I heard the faintest sound of a human voice. Heath looked to be waving and shouting, but the deafening roar of the waterfall drowned out his words. I waved back at him, before turning my attention to the task ahead.

The next two hops led me to within a few metres of his outstretched arms. I then kicked hard against the rock while letting the rope slip through the figure-of-eight. Suddenly I was airborne, while dropping past Heath's arms, straight into a pool of water. After surfacing, I let out an excited yell, then smiled up at Heath. By now, he was on his knees, reaching out to grab me. Instead of smiling, he was screaming out loud. 'Get out of the bloody water, mate. There's a tiger snake behind you!'

The thought of having one of the most venomous creatures in the world within arm's length hastened my speed from the water. Within seconds I was on the ledge, breathing hard, as Heath dragged me to safety, his voice raised above the roar of the falls. 'Didn't you hear me? I was waving at you to stop, but you've just dive-bombed one of the most dangerous creatures in the world.'

The snake was still close by and looked to be a metre long, its banded stripes impossible to miss, as it slid across the water with barely a ripple. While watching the snake, I called out to Heath. 'Just how poisonous are they?'

His reply brought me to my senses. 'Very poisonous, Alistair.'

I stepped back from the water's edge and turned to face him. 'What does *very* mean?'

'It means their venom is fatal, if not treated. They keep well away from people, but it appeared a moment ago. It was probably searching for frogs until you arrived on the scene.'

'If I'd have been bitten, how long would it have taken—'

'It's hard to say, but—'

Just then, Walter arrived by my side, camera in hand to capture a photo. 'Well done, Alistair. You've just survived a close encounter with a dangerous snake.'

He then reached out to help me unclip, as we watched the snake move away. It was swept unharmed towards an adjacent stream that cut a swathe through the trees. The guides soon called an end to the day's events, with the promise of a short trek to the minivan. During the drive back to Katoomba, Walter called out to me. 'Hey, Alistair, where did you learn to abseil?'

I explained about the time I'd learned the sport, while in the mountains of Andorra, many years earlier. He smiled in response, then turned his attention to our driver. 'Hey, Peter, I don't know about you, but I am very thirsty. I think it must be beer o'clock!'

Sometime later, I was seated in a bar with Walter and Kaioti. The other students had declined the offer of a drink, and our guides had left after one beer each, to prepare for another day.

By now, Walter seemed far mellower than the person I'd met outside the hostel that morning. Maybe it was due to the escapades in the canyon, or the sunset beers that had followed. While calling for a round of schnapps, he let slip that from time to time he became too competitive for his own good.

Then he said, 'I've enjoyed my time in the Blue Mountains, even if they are not very blue or as tall as the hills back home. I'm planning to head to Tasmania soon, to walk the Overland Track. Have you ever considered going there?'

'That's a worthy idea,' I said, 'but I need to chat with my wife first. She's in Romania at the moment and I think it's about time I called her.'

'Is she Romanian?' he asked, as I stood from the table.

'No, she's English, just like me. It's a bit of a long story, but I'll be back soon, to explain a little more.'

I made my way to a public phone and pulled an international calling card from my pocket. After punching in several numbers, I was rewarded with the faint sound of a ringing tone, followed by the voice of a man. 'Cine vorbeste te rog?'

I tried remembering the Romanian words that Fran had taught me over the years, but the long day and recent beers had clouded my thoughts. I gave it my best shot and said, 'Bună ziua, it's Alistair here. Is Francine there? Multumesc mult.'

The man on the end of the line let out a chuckle and said, 'Good try, Alistair. It's Gini here. How is Australia? I bet it is far warmer than here! At least Francine has warmed our hearts and we don't want to let her go. We have been reminiscing about all the work we did together at the orphanage, all those years ago. Here she is now. La revedere si mult noroc.'

The next voice was Fran's, but the crackled line meant I had to raise my voice to be heard. 'Hi Fran, what did he just say?'

'He wanted to wish you good luck. Gini and his family have been so helpful, especially as I turned up with little notice from Africa.'

The conversation soon turned to Fran's efforts to get the police clearance signed. 'Ali, it's minus five degrees and I've hardly spent anything, except to buy cigarettes and vodka for the police. I wanted to get some gloves but have been using socks on my hands instead. How about you? Have you been taking it easy on the budget?'

'You'd be proud of me, as I stayed in a dormitory for the first few days in Sydney.'

'Well done! I bet you loved every moment. Are you still in Sydney?'

'No, I'm in the Blue Mountains and don't want to leave. It's a pity you're not here.'

Fran's next words hit home for me. 'It's been lovely to rekindle old friendships, as they are all so caring and helpful, but I'm looking forward to being in Australia with you. With luck, I'll get the paperwork signed within a day or so.'

She then changed topic and asked, 'How was your day today? Have you been exploring the walking trails?'

'Well, I'm exhausted from canyoning and must have swallowed half a waterfall. I also had a close encounter with a tiger snake.'

'Oh, you are funny. Where are you now, as it seems very noisy?'

'I'm in a bar in Katoomba. You'd love it here.'

'Are you on your own?'

'No, I'm part of an international gathering, including a Japanese student and a German sports fanatic. Kaioti is gentle and hasn't stopped smiling all day. Walter is far more talkative.'

'It sounds as if I should know them both.'

'You might see Walter on TV one day, competing for Germany in the Winter Olympics.'

'What are you on about? Have you been drinking?'

'I've just had a few beers, followed by a peach schnapps.'

Fran soon brought me to my senses. 'Don't forget about Alice and Dave, as they arrive in Sydney anytime soon.'

The reunion with my brother and sister had been planned months earlier, with Alice flying in from London and Dave travelling interstate after months of travel. The aim had been for us all to enjoy the sights and sounds of Sydney together, but it now seemed likely that Fran would miss out on the first part, at least.

When she spoke next, her voice was quieter. 'Alice will be tired after such a long flight, but I know you'll look after her. Please give them both a hug from me. I'd so love to be there with you all. Where will you stay in Sydney?'

'I'm not sure yet, as I'm on the run from three crisp-crunching nerds from Northampton and don't want to end up in the same dormitory again.'

'Ali, I have no idea what you're talking about and haven't got the time right now. I'm off to the police station soon and need to get some warm clothes on.'

I wished her good luck and put down the phone, knowing that for Fran this would be a bittersweet time. Although I was looking forward to meeting up again, I felt a pang of guilt about the money just spent on excursions and drinks, while she prepared to head into the snow, wearing socks on her hands.

Walter and Kaioti were partway through their second schnapps by the time I returned. An hour later we walked out of the pub, in search of a karaoke bar. By now, the town was winding down for the night and apart from a late-night noodle bar, there was little on offer. Each of us chose the spicy noodles, and sat together on a park bench, reminiscing about the day in the canyon while sharing our favourite songs from back home. Twelve hours earlier, we'd been strangers to each other. Yet here we were, from different countries and cultures, sitting under the stars while talking gibberish, all a long way from home.

The following day was far more subdued. Walter left the hostel after breakfast to explore the trails, and the Japanese students returned to the city. I spent the morning browsing the shops before lounging away the afternoon in a funky café, enjoying teacakes and coffee while catching up on emails. That evening, I packed my bag in readiness for an early morning train ride to Sydney.

Somehow, the city seemed friendlier the second time round. The passengers nearest me played cards during the journey and their laughter became infectious. I stepped onto the platform with a spring in my step, despite the heavy pack on my back. I'd been carrying it for many months, and it had fared well across parts of South America and Africa.

I'd missed my family, but would soon have two siblings within touching distance. Dave was due to arrive first, and we'd arranged to meet in a pub close to the harbour. After booking into my third hostel in Sydney, I hesitantly made my way to the four-person dormitory. I opened the door to find a brightly lit room, with one unmade bunk bed. Although the sole occupant was out, he'd left a few clues regarding his hobbies and taste in food. Close to his bed I spotted a gardening magazine, alongside a bottle of mineral water! After a scout of the room, there was no sign of empty crisp packets or fizzy drinks on the spotless floor.

While humming a tune, I placed my rucksack on the nearest available bed and went in search of an internet café to check on Fran's progress. After logging onto my email account, I discovered she had sent a short, sweet message from Romania. It was titled, I'VE GOT IT... I'VE GOT IT... I'VE GOT IT.

I sat on the chair and studied the rest of the email, not quite believing what I was reading. She'd secured a police clearance and would be in Australia within a few days. With a beaming smile I turned to face the room, which was filled with travellers logged onto other computers. I then cleared my throat and raised my arms high before calling out. 'Ladies and gentlemen, I have an announcement to make. Thanks to the Romanian police force, I now have the opportunity to live in Australia with my wife. I'm off to the pub to celebrate.'

I ignored the blank looks and walked out of the café, punching the air and grinning, then headed into the city to meet my oldest brother. We met in The Rocks, known as the birthplace of modern Sydney, as early settlers from Europe forged new lives after arduous sea journeys lasting three to four months.

One pub which has stood the test of time is the Fortune of War, built in 1828 and famed as the oldest drinking den in Sydney. As I stepped inside the open plan bar, the first thing I noticed was a framed image on the nearest wall, depicting men in battle uniform, waiting to board ships.

It only took me a few moments to spot Dave amongst the lunchtime patrons. After months of travel on the open road, he looked tanned and relaxed, chatting with the barman as I approached. After hugs and handshakes, we ordered cold beers and sat close to the open windows to catch a breeze. I soon learned about his travels across parts of Africa and Australia and his plans for the future.

Alice arrived a day later, determined to enjoy her three-week escape from England. Nearing 50 but looking 40, she bounded into the hostel wearing a new pair of cargo pants and a red fleece jacket. Her fair hair had taken a battering during the long-haul journey and was hidden under a sea-blue, wide-brimmed hat. Despite the onset of jet lag, her eyes were bright as we warmly embraced and ventured into the city together.

By late afternoon, we were seated outside a waterside café, with commanding views of Sydney Opera House to our right and Sydney Harbour Bridge to our left. As we clinked glasses and raised them high, it struck me how varied our circumstances had become. Here we were, three siblings from England, all on different journeys.

Dave was on a quest for adventure, scaling many summits and diving coral reefs. He could recall every moment of his escapades, but after many months and numerous countries, his trip was nearly over, with a return to England looming closer.

Alice was seeking her own type of adventures, with time away from her husband and son, for a few valuable weeks. Working for an airline company meant she'd often enjoyed special deals to the Balearic Islands, but this was the first time she'd travelled so far alone. Now she was soaking up the last of the sunlight, staring across the water at a passing ferry, camera poised to capture the moment.

After we'd eaten, she headed to a nearby kiosk, returning minutes later with a panoramic postcard of Sydney harbour. With her pen poised for action, I asked, 'What are you going to write about, as you haven't really done much yet?'

She looked up with a tired smile and said, 'Of course I have. I've just flown halfway across the world, to enjoy a meal with two of my brothers, while looking over Sydney harbour. Besides, I enjoy writing postcards.'

It felt good to see her at ease, and as I strolled to the counter to order more drinks, Dave came with me. While we waited to be served, he pointed towards the Harbour Bridge. 'Can you see the headlamps of the climbers, Ali?'

I followed his gaze towards the darkening sky and stared up at the bridge. The infrastructure was dotted with many lights, including flashing beacons in specific locations, to ensure it didn't get hit by boats or low-flying aircraft. But there were also smaller lights moving across the catwalks and high beams.

By now, Alice had nearly finished her postcard. There was an inch of white space at the bottom and she looked to be pondering what to write next. I set down her wine and said, 'I've got an idea of how to finish the postcard. You could tell the folks back home what you're planning to do tomorrow.'

I pointed towards the faraway headlamps, which were now in a row, across the top of the bridge. 'See up there? That could be us, tomorrow. How do you fancy tackling the bridge climb?'

I was expecting some hesitation or a shake of the head. Instead, she giggled and said quietly, 'Okay, that sounds like fun.'

While we finished our drinks, Dave let slip that he'd climbed the bridge during a previous visit. He then said, 'I'm glad you're both giving it a go. You won't enjoy the cost, but the view from the top is spectacular.'

As if reading Alice's mind, he then added, 'It's very safe and no one has fallen off yet, apart from those who lost their lives during its construction.'

Alice peered over at the bridge, her eyes drooping from a lack of sleep. 'Well, I've come all this way, so I might as well give it a go.'

While back at the hostel, I made an online booking for two people. We were set to climb at midday on the following day. Once complete, I then scrolled through various websites to learn a little more about the bridge climb excursion and how it came to fruition.

The man to thank is an entrepreneur called Paul Cave. His interest in the bridge goes back to 1932, when his father-in-law purchased the first train ticket for the opening day of the railway line across the harbour.

Ticket number 00001 was later bequeathed to him after the death of his father-in-law and is now part of the memorabilia he collects regarding the bridge. In 1989, after nine months of negotiation and planning, he gained access to the upper section of the bridge for members of a Young Presidents Organisation. Following their successful climb, he then set in motion a two-year plan, to turn the concept into a tourist attraction.

At one point, he was given 62 reasons (by the government) why the venture would never work. In fact, it took nearly ten years to achieve his goal, but inch by inch, and dollar by dollar, he overcame every obstacle. Millions of people have now climbed the bridge, thanks to his vision and persistence.

Dave led the way to the entrance the following day and waved us goodbye for a few hours. Soon after, we were being introduced to Kate, our guide. She looked to be in her mid-twenties, with the physique of a long-distance runner and sharp blue eyes, which rarely strayed from the group of holidaymakers in front of her. We were a mixed group, including spotty teenagers, backpackers and sprightly retirees.

During the introduction, Kate gave away the age of her oldest climber to date, a woman in her early seventies. She then asked where we were all from. One couple had flown in from Brazil and a family of four from Singapore were planning to travel to the Great Barrier Reef by campervan.

The remaining climbers came from the UK, USA, Canada and Australia. Minutes earlier we'd all been breathalysed, and each of us had passed the mandatory test. Now we were in a brightly lit room, being kitted out with blue-and-grey boiler suits, which looked to be designed for comfort and safety rather than fashion.

Within a few hours, if all went well, we'd be standing on the top of Sydney Harbour Bridge, 134 metres above the water. Before commencing the safety briefing, Kate asked if we had any questions. She was initially met by silence, but one by one a few of the climbers found their voices.

'Has anyone ever fallen off?'

'Can I phone my mum from the top?'

'Can I use my camera during the climb?'

'What if I get scared and want to turn around?'

'What if I need to go to the toilet along the way?'

She answered each one swiftly and confidently. No doubt, she'd heard most of them before. After the questions had dried up, she then got into the detail. Throughout the climb we'd be tethered to a static line, by way of a safety harness. As the instructions continued, it became clear they'd considered every conceivable risk.

Nothing was being left to chance. Pockets were emptied, hair clips removed, jewellery coaxed off and watches unstrapped. Cameras and phones received the same treatment and before we left, all items were locked away.

Although Alice smiled while Kate called her forward to check her harness, I knew she'd be feeling anxious. A nervous giggle was all she let show, as we took our first steps onto a wide beam above the busy roadway. Cars whizzed past, just below our feet, followed soon after by a slow-moving train, drowning out the excited squeals from the front climber.

We moved at a steady pace, along catwalks framed by steel barriers, and then made our way up a series of metal steps. While gaining height, we spotted sailing boats, carving their way across the wide harbour. Occasionally, we noticed other climbers up ahead, their dark shapes silhouetted against the bright sky.

Just after the halfway point, Kate stopped close to the edge and asked us to look down. Through gaps in the steel columns, stairwells and sturdy mesh, we could see the dappled water, washing against the infrastructure.

She then called us to attention and began reeling off a few facts and figures. 'During the construction of the bridge between 1923 and 1932, about 1,400 workers were employed, including engineers, boilermakers, carpenters, crane drivers and labourers. Out of these, sixteen workers lost their lives because of workplace accidents. Only two workers survived a fall into the water. One of those was an Irishman called Vincent Kelly, who fell 55 metres after slipping from the decking. For those of you who understand imperial measurements, that's around 180 feet.'

Kate gave us a few seconds to absorb this information, before continuing with the story. 'It's said that during his fall, he completed a somersault and landed feet first.'

While we stood side by side, Kate raised her voice and completed the tale. 'The force of the impact was so great that the soles of his boots were ripped to shreds and he also suffered multiple rib fractures. Mind you, he was back at work within six weeks!'

Throughout the rest of the climb, I couldn't stop thinking about Vincent Kelly. Would the construction workers at the time ever have believed that future visitors would pay hundreds of dollars to be escorted to the top of the bridge? Unlike us, they wouldn't have had safety harnesses, or the chance of a photo taken at the top by a digital camera, secured to the infrastructure.

I still have the photo of Alice and me, standing side by side during that sunny afternoon. By the time we'd reached the top, her fears had vanished, replaced by a wide smile and many questions for Kate about all that lay before us. Most eyes were drawn towards the white-tiled roof of Sydney Opera House, far in the distance, but there was so much more to see.

The harbour was alive with colour and noise. While Kate spoke, I heard the faint sound of a horn blasting three times in succession. Two ferries were in transit across the water, heading between the beachside suburbs. If those on board were to look up, they'd see many ant-like figures standing in a line across the top of the bridge.

Just before Kate ushered us from the top, I gazed inland. Out there, beyond the city centre, was a sunburned interior, steeped in history and filled with mystery. Fran was due to return from Romania any day soon, and we'd made plans to meet her in the outback. After that, who knew? Maybe we'd explore Tasmania together before returning to the mainland and spending time in the historic laneways of Melbourne.

After the climb, we met up with Dave for a visit to Sydney Olympic Park, where the summer Olympics of 2000 took place. Each of us had bathers and after paying the entrance fee, took a swim in the Olympic-sized pool. Dave challenged me to a 50-metre race and won by half a length while Alice sat by the side with her legs in the water, laughing at my doggy paddle strokes.

After being beaten, I turned my attention to starting block number four and swam towards it. An Australian Olympian called Ian Thorpe had once stood on the same raised platform. In front of thousands of spectators and millions of TV viewers, he produced a perfect dive, before swimming for gold in the 400-metre freestyle, in a world record time of 3:40:59.

I called out to Alice about the history of lane four and watched as she stepped onto the starting block. After a nervous glance at the deep pool of water, she inched towards the edge and called out, 'I think I might try a dive, but I've never done one before. What do you think?'

'Go on,' I replied, while treading water close by. 'It's now or never.'

While I waited with bated breath, Alice pressed her palms together, with arms outstretched and knees bent. The dive that followed produced an almighty splash as she belly-flopped into the water and spluttered to the surface. Although it wouldn't have scored many points from an Olympic judge, Dave and I both agreed that the heroic dive had been the highlight of our visit.

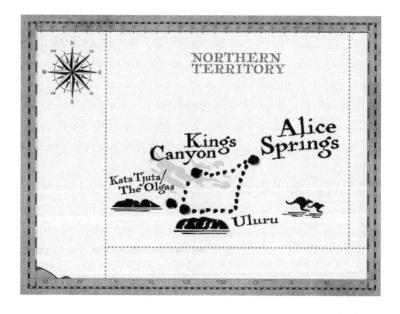

From Sydney, we flew to the Northern Territory for a taste of the outback and as expected, met my friend, Mark. He'd also taken the redundancy payout from General Motors and had been travelling for many months.

The flies were waiting as we emerged from the air-conditioned plane and made our way down the steps. All thoughts of getting a photo alongside the *Welcome to Alice Springs* sign disappeared, as I fought off buzzing insects and searched for the doorway into the terminal. After collecting our luggage from the conveyor, we stepped outside again, in search of Mark.

I was still flapping my hands in front of my face when he appeared, seemingly unaffected by the black haze around us. Blessed with an enviable mop of blonde hair, now bleached by the sun, it was clear that extensive travelling suited him well. With an easy-going swagger, he helped Alice with her luggage and led us towards the hired car.

In contrast to the face-painted Aboriginals I'd encountered at Circular Quay in Sydney, dressed in traditional costume while playing the didgeridoo to tourists, those in Alice Springs seemed less exuberant. Like us, they wore shorts, T-shirts and sandals as they wandered around the town centre.

How the town got its name is worth sharing. In 1871, an English surveyor by the name of William Whitfield Mills was studying the local terrain to find the best route for a telegraph line to pass through the area. He was involved in a challenging project to connect Adelaide, in the country's south, with Palmerston (Darwin) in the north.

During this time, he discovered local tribes using a series of waterholes which he assumed were springs, when in fact they were part of a river system. He named the settlement as Alice Springs, after the wife of Charles Todd, the man tasked with managing the engineering project.

The immense task of constructing the telegraph line included the addition of eleven repeater stations, positioned at intervals between 200 to 290 kilometres. The total length of the line was estimated to be 3,200 kilometres long, through desert, flood plains and mountainous regions. Charles Todd was given the honour of sending the first message on the line and did so in October 1872, with these words:

'We have this day, within two years, completed a line of communications two thousand miles long through the very centre of Australia, until a few years ago a terra incognita believed to be a desert.'

By now, I was keen to get in contact with Fran again, as it had been two weeks since we'd gone our separate ways. During the previous 24 hours, she'd flown from Romania to England, then headed to Australia via Singapore. After touching down in Sydney, she then flew to Ayers Rock, which sits in the middle of Australia, five hours' drive from the nearest major town, Alice Springs.

The black bitumen shimmered under the midday sun as we drove across the desert in air-conditioned bliss. Our destination was Ayers Rock Resort, which is operated in conjunction with the local Aboriginal community to create synergy between indigenous groups and the hospitality sector.

The receptionist directed us to Fran's room, which was hidden amongst rows of cabins set out in the manicured gardens. The block of units hummed steadily as overworked air conditioners battled against the oppressive heat. Her door cracked open, flooding the room with light, to reveal a creature from the night. But the crumpled pyjamas and dishevelled blonde hair could only be Fran's. Through yawns and hugs, she described the bitter cold of an East European winter and the forgotten relationships unexpectedly stirred to life.

I interrupted her emotional recollections to say, 'Fran, we're really interested in what happened in Romania, but time is pressing. It will soon be sunset, and according to our guide-book, Ayers Rock will stir to life in an explosion of colour.'

The heat rose to her cheeks as she replied, 'Well, Ali, for starters, its official name is now Uluru, not Ayers Rock. It might burst into colour and I hope to be there, but I'm ready to drop after such a long journey. While you've been gallivant-ing around Sydney, I've been traipsing around Romania in tem-peratures of minus five degrees, trying to bribe a police captain with vodka and cigarettes. I did all of this, so we could get a visa to live and work in Australia.'

Then the tone of her voice shifted, as she said, 'Actually, it was so that *you* could get a visa. This was your plan all along, not mine. I'm happy to go back to England. I'm tired, hot, and smelly and you're all staring at me!'

I smiled and held her tightly in a long-overdue hug. Fifteen minutes later she was showered and dressed. As we made our way towards the hired vehicle, I cast my eyes to the cloudless sky, hoping we wouldn't be too late for the sunset.

For years, the 348-metre monolith was known as Ayers Rock, after the former chief secretary of South Australia, Sir Henry Ayers. But in 1993, the iconic sight became one of the first natural landmarks to regain its Aboriginal name and is now regarded as Uluru. This term relates not only to the rock but also to the surrounding terrain. Travellers are attracted to this remote area of central Australia in the hope of capturing the special moment when the rock changes colour during sun-rise and sunset.

We drove to the designated parking area, where rows of cars and minibuses signalled the official viewing location and tourists waited patiently for the sun to set. Uluru could be seen from afar, its steep sides and flattened top standing proud against the pale sky.

Once out of the car, we were greeted by persistent flies. The smartest of travellers had arrived with fly nets and stood nearby, taking photos without the distraction of waving the insects away. Those without fly nets snapped quickly, or held their cameras with one hand while shooing flies away with the other.

The light faded and the frustrating black plague diminished, just as the rock momentarily flushed. The colour of the contoured slopes changed from murky brown to autumn leaves, and for a few minutes, a hazy red. Then the moment was over and the symbolic rock became a dark outline on the fading horizon.

Maybe we were tired after months of travel and not appreciative of one of the natural wonders of the world, but the sunset failed to inspire. Uluru sunsets can be memorable, but nature doesn't always comply. It just so happened that the one we had just witnessed was easy on the eye, but far from endearing.

Back at camp, Fran regained her composure after overrunning the quota of hot water usage in the communal showers. We then headed to the outdoor bar where a travelling musician sang for his supper under a clear night sky. Scared of missing out on a stunning sunrise, we forced ourselves out of bed in the chilly pre-dawn, although Dave decided he'd seen enough sunrises and rolled over for more sleep.

A convoy of hired cars left camp, searching for the lookout point to witness the event. After arriving, we stood in a ragged line alongside many other tourists, cameras at the ready. A glint of sunlight appeared on the horizon, signalling a dawn chorus of waking parrots that filled the air, as the rock came to life in the early light.

The mood of Uluru altered as the rising sun flushed the steep sides, turning them lilac, then pink, and for a few seconds a vibrant red. Alice was lost in the moment, either taking photos or absorbed in the transition from night to day. While walking across to Fran, I noticed a subtle change in the light and returned my focus towards Uluru. The sun was above the horizon and the moment had gone.

As we packed up and prepared to leave, Mark stretched an arm across my shoulders. 'Not bad, Ali. Not bad at all. Let's wake up Dave, to tell him what he's missed.'

By mid-morning we were on the road to view 36 giant domes of red rock, known as The Olgas. The landmark is also known as Kata Tjuta, meaning 'many heads' and is sacred to the local Aboriginal people, who have inhabited the area for over 20,000 years. Upon first sighting, they appealed to my sense of adventure, looming high above the desert, each one a different shape and size to the next.

We soon discovered a network of trails, which gave us the chance to walk amongst the steep sided mounds. While clambering over rounded boulders in search of shade, we spotted rock wallabies. Although smaller than kangaroos, they hopped with speed to keep their distance, heading deeper into the shadows. Despite the allure and isolation of Kata Tjuta, the heat and flies won the day, forcing us back to our car. Along the way, I stopped to admire the surrounds, including the highest point, Mount Olga, reaching 546 metres above the desert floor.

After returning to the comforts of our room and taking a swim in the pool, a late afternoon trek was planned around the base of Uluru. This time, we wore fly nets and took enough water to last for hours as we circumnavigated the huge rock along an easy trail. At times, we stopped to admire nooks and curves in the ancient rock and stopped to chat with tourists heading the other way. Like us, they were on the lookout for rock art, wallabies and waterholes. Although our search was unsuccessful, the 10-kilometre walk had raised a sweat and in celebration we sat that evening by the poolside bar, listening to the same musician sing for their supper.

Once more, we woke to clear skies and during a leisurely breakfast studied our road map, with plans to leave by midday. Our next destination was Kings Canyon, four hours' drive away, across flat, arid plains. Before setting off, we loaded up with snacks and water, in preparation for a six-kilometre trek around the rim of the canyon.

Throughout the afternoon walk, we never encountered anyone else and stopped at intervals to admire the bird's-eye view of the surrounding desert. By sunset, the sandstone walls of the canyon came to life, prompting a flurry of photos as each of us tried capturing the moment. In the last of the light, Alice took a few tentative steps towards the 100-metre ledge, her shadow stretching far across the blazing canyon.

After a cosy night in a budget motel close to the canyon, we loaded up the car and drove across the desert to Alice Springs. That afternoon, while Fran packed our luggage to prepare for interstate flights, I took a walk from our hostel, in search of an internet café. Within a few clicks of the keyboard, I was rewarded with a simple message from the Australian authorities. They'd processed the police clearance from Romania, which meant that our application for visas had been granted.

Many months earlier, I'd stood on the Vauxhall factory floor and watched people's lives change forever as they realised the car plant would shut down. That moment had taken me to a backstreet café, in the middle of the Australian desert.

I soon found myself grinning at every passer-by as I raced back to the hostel. Because of Australian law, you cannot gain residency if you are already in the country. This would mean a trip abroad to visit an overseas Australian consulate for passport stamping. I met Mark in the reception area and spilled the news. For over a decade, we'd shared our dreams and aspirations. As he shook my hand, I thought back to the long nights at the car factory, when we'd spent our free time studying textbooks, rather than reading tabloids.

The following morning, we hugged at the airport, as he followed his dreams, and we followed ours. He was travelling to Queensland in search of scuba-diving activities and the rest of us to the cosmopolitan metropolis of Melbourne. After the Qantas flight levelled out, I went in search of the nearest crew member to run an idea past them. A few minutes later, the stewardess gave a special announcement over the intercom. 'Ladies and gentlemen, please welcome Australia's newest residents, Alistair and Francine, seated in row nine. I hope they accept our offer of a bottle of champagne, to enjoy during the flight to Melbourne.'

I couldn't imagine such a warm welcome anywhere else and smiled as Fran topped up our glasses and Alice wiped away a tear. During the descent into Melbourne, I pinned my face to the nearby window and stared out at the sprawling suburbs, reaching far into the distance. There were houses everywhere, close together, unless segregated by busy roads or pockets of greenery. I also spotted swimming pools in gardens, but as the plane flew lower, the houses gave way to train lines, factories, and shopping centres surrounded by car parks.

Although the city was far bigger than I'd envisaged, it soon revealed its cultural heart. The weather reminded me of home, with plenty of clouds and a cool wind, but no one seemed too bothered. The city centre looked industrious, with many shoppers and office workers in transit across the pavements or bunched at intersections, waiting for the lights to change. Trams trundled along the busy streets, stopping occasionally at designated bays to collect, or eject, their passengers. By late afternoon, restaurants and wine bars began to fill, as office workers arrived on the scene, in search of a drink before heading home.

Melbourne is famous for its bustling laneways, which are found throughout the city centre and offer the chance to enjoy street art, along with a myriad of culinary delights. That evening, we explored a few of the narrow laneways and jostled for space alongside city dwellers and overseas travellers. Some walked casually, arm in arm, while others sat around tables, enjoying the chance for alfresco dining.

Each laneway had a different vibe from the last. In one, it was all about the music, with guitar players and classical singers performing in open-plan bars. We stopped for a while, enjoyed a glass of wine and soon this turned into another, followed by tapas at a Spanish restaurant.

One reason for the trip to Melbourne was for Alice and Dave to visit some of their relatives. We have the same mother, but I have a different father and they were here to visit their dad's family. The following day, emotional hugs were dished out by Mary, Martin and Anne Marie, as they welcomed us into their family home.

Their rural property lies just out of reach of Melbourne's urban sprawl, allowing them to lead a country life, complete with cows, pigs and a retired sheep dog. Tea and scones magically appeared on the dining room table, but after another top-up, Martin pulled up a chair and sat alongside me. Although he'd spent more of his life in Australia than Ireland, he hadn't lost the distinct accent. In a soft Irish brogue, he said, 'Ali, I need to find some missing cattle. Do you fancy giving me a hand?'

While Alice and Dave received a family history lesson, Martin drove me along quiet country roads, past waterways, train lines and paddocks. During the trip, he explained that the cattle were his way of keeping busy during retirement. It struck me that he seemed perfectly happy with his hobby and during the drive he explained the differences between each breed and the latest market price for a healthy bullock.

We soon found the broken fence, which he temporarily repaired, before resuming the search, this time on foot. I expected to do a lot of things in Melbourne, but chasing cattle across low-lying fields was not one of them. Hours later, we returned home victorious, with all the livestock safely rounded up.

The following morning, I contacted a friend called Vince who'd moved to Melbourne from my hometown in England, many years before. We arranged to meet in a city-centre pub.

Just before the call ended, Vince said, 'Don't forget to wrap up warm, as I'm taking you all to watch the footy at the MCG.'

Australians refer to their most popular spectator sport as 'the footy' and if you are going to watch an *Australian Rules* football match, there is no better place than the Melbourne Cricket Ground. From humble beginnings in 1853, the ground has undergone major developments over the years and is now considered one of Australia's most iconic landmarks. The vast grandstand accommodates 100,000 spectators and is ringed by six lighting towers reaching 85 metres. The cricket ground is also used to host the football grand final each year.

Before we headed into the city, I sat with Anne Marie to understand the rules and history of the game. First, she asked, 'So, Ali, which team does your mate support?'

'I've no idea. Melbourne, I suppose.'

She leaned back in her chair and rolled her eyes. 'Alistair, you have so much to learn about footy. We have ten professional teams in the state of Victoria, and most of these are based in Melbourne. Those with any sense support the Bombers. Well, that's their nickname. Their official name is Essendon Football Club.'

She then leant forward and dropped her voice. 'I'm afraid there are those within our family who have been drawn towards the dark side. They support the Tigers, but I don't like to talk about Richmond Football Club too much.'

On a chilly March evening, we wrapped up to join tens of thousands to cheer on Vince's favourite team, which we soon learned were the Tigers. The players wore black football tops with a yellow stripe angled across the front and back. The opposing team, Collingwood, was also from Melbourne, which made for a near sell-out crowd.

Despite Anne Marie's earlier attempt to teach me the rules, I quickly realised that I didn't understand what was going on. This didn't stop me from settling into my seat to enjoy the spectacle. The game turned out to be fast-paced, with flair ups, the occasional tussle, a few ripped shirts and a bloody nose for one gangly defender.

Throughout the brawls, bumps and tackles, the ball kept moving, resulting in a flurry of goals from both sides. It soon became clear to me that unlike the world game, once played by the likes of David Beckham, Aussie Rules is a high-scoring event–with the winning team notching up 94 goals!

During the on-field antics and constant goals, there was little banter between the opposing fans, which surprised me, but the packed stadium still created a lively atmosphere. At half time, Vince led us to a busy kiosk and treated us to pie and chips, which we washed down with cold beers.

The sport reminded me of Gaelic football, but instead of a round ball, they used an oval one. It also had a major advantage over the type of football I was used to watching. Being such a high-scoring spectacle, it was possible to duck to the toilet during the match, without worrying about the chance of missing a vital goal.

The following day, Dave flew back to England with truckloads of fresh stories. This was my big brother. When would I see him again? His life was in England and mine was on hold. Alice stayed on to explore a little more of Australia and joined us for the one-hour flight to Tasmania.

After hiring a car, and with no set itinerary or plan, we took to the open road and quickly fell in love with the island. Tasmania has the appeal of being isolated from the mainland, while being blessed with ancient forests, lush hillsides and wide rivers. Its southern latitude has blessed the island with a temperate climate, which surprises those expecting all parts of Australia to be sun-baked. Although the island makes up only one percent of Australia's total landmass, it receives 12 percent of the rain.

Tasmanians are more used to wearing thermals than swimwear, but untamed forests, craggy mountains and an unspoilt coastline add to the island's character and appeal. The wheat-growing areas of mainland Australia have seen fluctuations in rainfall and Tasmania looks set to take advantage, with many older farms being snapped up by multinationals. Strategists now look at this emerald isle as Australia's premier food supplier for the future.

Each bend in the road revealed something new to behold. We spotted farm buildings in the shadow of steep hills and crossed feisty streams, meandering towards pockets of woodland. There were few cars, no chance of road rage and too many panoramic viewpoints to choose from. Away from the coast there seemed to be more livestock than people, and while passing remote farms we often received friendly waves from those at work.

The tranquil seaside town of Bicheno proved to be a delightful spot for Fran and Alice to terrorise the chatty barman of the seafront pub, who offered to teach them the technicalities of playing pool. I knew they'd soon drive him to despair and took a stroll on a nearby beach while they played. The windswept shore, with its rock pools, ice-blue water and wading birds, reminded me of a similar scene, in the west coast of Ireland. By the time I returned, the barman had taken a fancy to Alice, but we were on a whirlwind tour and I whisked her away.

The remaining days flew past in a haze as we circumnavigated the island and briefly explored the wild and isolated southwest region. Some parts of this wilderness are known to be 50 kilometres from the nearest road, but we played it safe and rarely ventured far from the car. Large tracts of woodland are still relatively unexplored, and there are those who hope the Tasmanian tiger still exists within the protected environment.

The animal's name is derived from the dark stripes across its lower back. But it was actually a thylacine, not a tiger. These large carnivorous marsupials once numbered over 5,000, but for many reasons, including habitat loss and hunting, their numbers dwindled during the late nineteenth century. In 1888, the Tasmanian government introduced a bounty for each dead animal, and for the price of a pound, their fate was all but sealed.

The last known shooting occurred in 1930, and by the time they were given protected status, it was too late. The last captive thylacine died in Beaumaris Zoo in 1936, after being trapped in bushland and transported to Hobart. Tasmanian tiger sightings continue to this day, but somehow the photos and video footage always seem to be out of focus or shaky. I know it is wishful thinking but I hope they are still out there, deep in the remaining forests, staying out of sight until we learn to respect them!

One location that proved easy to find was Cradle Mountain, located further north, in the Tasmanian Wilderness World Heritage Area. This UNESCO World Heritage Site is over three million acres in size and is filled with temperate forests, alpine plateaus and craggy hills. Cradle Mountain lies at the heart, luring trekkers to experience a wilderness bush walk from its base to Lake St Clair, six days away by foot.

We ventured onto the overland track for an afternoon ramble towards the jagged outline of the distant peak, but had ran out of time to embrace this stunning location. Alice was booked on a flight to the UK and our memorable time on this diverse island ended on the lower slopes of the windswept mountain.

Back at Melbourne airport, tears rolled as we bade farewell to Alice. As my only sister, she'd always been there for me over the years. We were like best friends. Why was I leaving my family? Our decision to move to Australia was proving to be an emotional one. Alice disappeared through the gate marked *Singapore* and once again, Fran and I were on our own.

To get our visas, we also needed to leave the country. We chose Fiji, because it was a new location for us both, and only five hours away. After watching Alice's plane head into the clouds, we made our way towards the departure lounge, just in time to hear the last call. It was time to get our passports stamped!

Island in the Sun

"Adventure is just bad planning."
  – Roald Amundsen

As soon as we touched down at Nadi International Airport, I felt a surge of excitement at the prospect of exploring parts of Viti Levu, Fiji's largest island. I was also keen to travel to neighbouring islands, but first we had work to do regarding our passports.

A threatening band of black clouds gathered overhead, as we made our way across the tarmac in search of our luggage and a taxi to Suva. Three hours later, the driver dropped us off at the gates of the South Seas Hotel, a whitewashed building with wide corridors and high ceilings, filled with whirring fans that attempted to recirculate the oppressive air.

Most room doors were open in the hope of catching a breeze and many residents were lying on their beds, or in the case of our new neighbour, standing in the middle of his room while attempting a challenging yoga posture. This wasn't a place for backpackers, but a hotel for transients. The heat and humidity seemed to have sucked the life out of most of the guests. Some ambled along the corridors, while others fussed in the kitchen over noodles and stir-fries.

Nightfall brought a welcome relief from the humidity, although fatigue robbed us of anything too energetic. After an evening stroll, we opted for fish curry at a roadside café, followed by an early night and a final peek to check on our nimble neighbour.

Eight hours later, a stream of light slipped through a gap in the curtains, signalling our big day was about to begin. I shook Fran gently and whispered, 'Wake up, it's time to get our passports stamped.'

She opened her eyes and said, 'This doesn't mean it's permanent, does it? We can always go back to England, can't we? Remember what we said–it's just an adventure.'

At midday, we stepped out of a taxi, wearing the smartest clothes we could muster, and headed into the marbled foyer of the Australian High Commission. The doorman ushered us into a large waiting room adorned with a bank of ceiling fans, which did little to ease the humidity.

We sat in the corner and studied the faces of those waiting nearby. Some looked calm and composed, while others fidgeted in their seats or paced the room. Thirty minutes later, an official called us to the counter to relinquish our passports. The female clerk greeted us with a smile, then slipped a hand through the generous gap of the security screen to collect our documents. As she headed into a back room with a promise to return soon, Fran held my hands tight.

'Ali, I'm nervous. What if they say no?'

I attempted a serious face and said, 'Well, they might deny yours, but I should be okay. You could come and visit me once a year.'

The clerk walked back into view, handed over the documents and waited patiently for a polite response. After many months of uncertainty, we were speechless and sat awkwardly, holding our unopened passports.

Together, we searched for the stamp of approval in each document. Fran was first to find a blue stamp with the words 'Permanent Visa' etched across a watermarked page. Moments later, I flicked open my passport to discover a freshly stamped page with the same two words. Finally, we could find a place to live and work in Australia.

While we sat admiring the documents, the clerk stayed put, waiting for a reaction, realising that our silence was due to a mixture of relief and elation. Fran stirred to life and reached out to squeeze the clerk's slender hands. 'Thank you, thank you,' she whispered.

We wanted to jump over the counter, hug her senseless and gift her with flowers. But all we had to offer was wide smiles and awkward handshakes. As we fussed by the counter and thanked her again, a straight-faced security guard came to life and began approaching. We took this as a signal to leave and walked out of the embassy, waving to the smiling clerk as we crossed the polished floor in search of champagne.

I called my dad from a public phone box in Suva, to tell him the news. Despite the static on the line, I sensed his approval as he asked, 'Where are you now?'

'We're in Suva, Dad. It's in Fiji.'

His voice boomed down the wire. 'Och aye, I know Suva well. I had a girlfriend there many years ago, after I jumped ship and stayed on the island for a while. It was before I married your mum, of course.'

'Dad, why is it I only ever hear these stories at the most bizarre times? I know so little about what you were like back then.'

'Ah, son, I'll tell you the full story one day. We used to visit a bar near the harbour. It had a blue roof and an outdoor dance floor. You should go there to celebrate.'

The chances of it still being open were near impossible after all these years, but I didn't mention this to my dad. I was just glad to be hearing a snippet of his wayward travels as a merchant sailor. I waited a few moments and said, 'Love you lots. Don't forget, this winter you're staying with us in Australia. You promised, remember?'

'We'll see. I'm getting too old for long distance travel. My back's playing up and my passports out of date. Anyhow, say hi to Fran. I'm off to play golf.'

We went in search of champagne but ended up in a roadside bar, sipping beer while enjoying fish curry. During a search for the toilet, Fran noticed a sign on the wall, advertising beachside cabins on the nearby island of Caqalai. By the following morning, we were heading out to sea.

We'd been picked up at the quayside by the island caretaker, who gave his name as Joseph while reaching out to shake our hands. He looked to be about 40, with wide shoulders, ruffled hair and green eyes. His simple wooden boat was powerful enough to propel us into the Moturiki passage, where a passing shower obscured all visibility. The vessel led us through the mist, slicing through white crests and navigating the swells towards our waiting island.

During the crossing I tried making small talk, but Joseph's focus remained on the waters ahead. I soon took his cue and watched the ocean for signs of land. We emerged from the rain into bright sunshine, and our first sighting of a low-lying island, sitting on the distant horizon.

A choir of women and children, standing ankle-deep in the clear water, greeted us with cheery smiles. They waved and sang as our craft skirted a rocky outcrop and banked on the sand. One child took Fran's hand to lead us to our Fijian *bure*, a wooden cabin that housed a double bed protected by a mosquito net. The window was open, revealing a breathtaking view, as two coconut trees bowed towards a crescent of pure white sand, lapped by crystal blue water.

Positioned between each tree was a string hammock, stirring in the breeze. While Fran tested out the hammock, I counted the distance from our cabin to the South Pacific Ocean. As my toes touched the warm water, I called out, 'It's 12 steps from our bed to the ocean. What do you think about that?'

Before she could reply, we heard a sound that resembled a trumpet being blown. It was repeated a few seconds later, the low-pitched note hard to ignore. We heeded its call, and within a few minutes came face to face with Joseph, standing outside his home alongside a handful of other guests. He was holding a conch and smiling widely. 'Welcome, everyone. We don't have phones on the island, but are lucky enough to have large seashells. When used as an instrument, they're perfect for calling everyone together.'

The house had a communal patio, used each evening for supper and decorated with lighted candles, fanned by a welcome sea breeze. The wholesome dinner of crab curry, grilled tuna and locally grown vegetables proved to be a perfect compliment to the bottles of wine smuggled over by two young women from Melbourne, who were happy to share their booty.

There were other diners among us, including a French backpacker named Marie. We soon discovered that she was our neighbour, in the adjacent bure, five coconut trees away! The most talkative guest was a man called Bob, on holiday from Brisbane. Without prompting, he soon shared that he'd been visiting the island for many years. He looked to be in his sixties, with a slick of grey hair and a mouth that refused to stay closed for long. From time to time, Joseph would wait for silence and then try to explain his role on the island, but Bob would often beat him to it.

Between them both, I learned the island is managed by the Methodist Church and caters to a maximum of 40 guests. We'd arrived during a quiet period–just a group of 12, with no one else booked in the days ahead.

While Bob excused himself for a toilet break, Joseph elaborated on his role as caretaker and the duties his family undertook. They were expected to cook for the guests and share some Fijian traditions, including weaving, fishing and the drinking of kava. While we tucked into our dessert, he passed around a pepper plant and explained how the root is crushed to produce kava powder. Once mixed with water, it then becomes a medicinal and therapeutic drink, often used during social functions across the Pacific region.

He also explained the different meanings of the term, *Bula*. In most cases, it is a friendly greeting, in the same way that I would say *hello*. At other times, it can mean *life*, or *to live*, or when drinking kava, can mean *cheers*.

On Sunday morning, we accepted an invitation to church, which also meant dressing up. Joseph took one look at my crumpled T-shirt and shorts, before escorting me to his home to try on a selection of sulus. Mine resembled a Scottish kilt, without the tartan. While I tried it on, Joseph explained that sulus were introduced to Fijians during the days of colonisation and were still popular on special occasions.

His wife applied the magic touch by tucking and pleating the lime-green outfit, to ensure I looked presentable for the Sunday service. Fran received the same treatment but looked far more graceful as she climbed on board the boat and called for me to join her. Our destination was the village of Niubasaga, on the island of Moturiki, a few miles away.

A few other visitors joined us for the 30-minute boat journey, across one of the straits separating the multitude of coral islands and outlying reefs. I sat next to Joseph, eager to watch how he operated the vessel. He returned my scrutiny with a knowing smile, his eyes rarely diverting from the waters ahead. After we'd anchored on a wide stretch of beach, Joseph's wife hitched up her cotton shawl and jumped onto the soft sand. We all followed suit, as she headed for a scattering of distant trees that hid the neat white church.

We were greeted at the doorway by a jolly faced minister, adorned in a long white robe and sandals. Although he had the solid build of a rugby player, his handshake was gentle as he guided me and Fran to the front row seats. He then turned his attention to the next arrivals, greeting many on first-name terms.

As expected, the congregation sang their hearts out to the Lord, standing tall in the packed aisles. Each hymn sounded louder than the last, with those nearby reaching high-pitched notes which resonated throughout the building. I spent most of the animated sermon fiddling with my sulu, which kept threatening to unravel each time we stood for hymns.

As the sermon ended, the congregation hushed and left the church in an orderly fashion, shaking hands with the minister along the way. Any thoughts of a Sunday afternoon chat between friends were cut short, as a stiff wind and angry clouds dispersed the crowd. Most of the congregation made a dash inland, towards a nearby village beyond the trees.

Our family marched across a wide sandbar towards the boat. We launched into the stirring sea, with all eyes on the mottled clouds that had descended on the bay. The temperature dropped as a cool wind tore across the water, followed by a horizontal torrent of rain, which drenched every passenger.

Joseph remained calm and guided the boat through choppy waters. For a few moments the boat pitched awkwardly, as the wind tossed us against the growing swell. Most passengers sat low on the deck, either to stabilise the boat or to shelter from the spray. Fran and I huddled together while crouching low as Joseph steered us through the rain.

The dark clouds dispersed, revealing our island on the horizon, and the boat eased gently towards the welcome shoreline. Joseph seemed unaffected by the turbulent passage, and his seamanship had impressed me. He seemed to be a man of many talents, acting as island caretaker, tourist guide, boat keeper and fisherman.

I went over to thank him and in reply, he said, 'I'm glad you came to church with us. The return crossing was a little rough, but tomorrow's weather should be calm and sunny. I'm going fishing in the morning, if you want to join me.'

'Yes, please. That sounds amazing. What time do you want me? Just after sunrise, I suppose.'

He shook his head and smiled. 'No, I need my breakfast first and besides, the fish aren't going anywhere.'

As planned, we launched the boat soon after breakfast. The sun was just beginning to bite, but Joseph didn't seem fazed as he started the engine and waved to his family. We were soon chugging through the glassy water, leaving behind a creamy wake as he navigated around a network of reefs while heading towards a rocky outcrop known as Snake Island.

After days of near silence, he finally started chatting, his green eyes sparkling as he talked about life on the island and the abundance of fish in his secret spots. He'd stripped down to a pair of shorts, and looked tanned and fit, with little sign of middle-age spread. His unkempt hair was mostly hidden under a bush hat bleached by the sun. As we skirted another reef, his eyes darted left, drawn to a movement under the water. He pushed the tiller, throttled the motor and called out, 'Get ready, Alistair. Can you see the fish?'

Before I had time to look over the side, he gave me a series of quick-fire instructions. 'Throw the net out. Quickly now. That's good, keep going. Watch it doesn't catch. Hurry please, a few are escaping.'

The ocean looked to be bubbling, maybe from the propeller churn or the captured fish thrashing around. After cutting the engine, he called out for me to jump overboard, to investigate our catch. I swam around the far side of the net, watching a school of silvery fish whipping in a tight circle. One part of the net had folded, showing signs of a struggle. Joseph watched from the boat and called out a warning. 'Be careful–it could be a barracuda and their teeth are razor sharp.'

The net had wrapped around its body, causing it to thrash until exhausted. Some fish had caught their gills in the net, and these were the ones that Joseph wanted first. I handpicked each one, before throwing them into his cupped hands.

I felt compelled to free a few, guiding them through gaps or placing them over the top of the net, until Joseph caught me. He laughed out loud and said, 'Hey, Alistair, leave my dinner alone.'

After I'd climbed back on board, we pulled the net in together. The barracuda slid to the deck, twitching a few times before laying lifeless. I picked it up by the tail, admiring the steely blue skin and pointed teeth. It was longer than my arm and far superior to any of the other catch.

While stowing the net, he said, 'We've been lucky today, but nothing will go to waste. There's one more place I'd like to try before we head back.' He then handed me a fishing spear and said, 'Put on your mask and follow me to the bottom. You can try to get a fish, but if you haven't done it before, it will be hard.'

After anchoring the boat, he then dived below the water, armed with his own spear while wearing a diving mask. I tried following, but my lungs quickly complained, forcing me to the surface. I bobbed patiently, happy to tread water, and watched as he disappeared into an underwater cave to spear an unknown creature. His powerful legs pushed him deeper, forcing air bubbles to the surface as the hunt continued below. He emerged from the depths, holding a pan-sized fish, which twitched and struggled as he pulled the jagged spear from its leathery skin.

With tonight's menu completed, we headed back to the island for a fish banquet. As the boat came to rest in the shallows, I stood knee-deep in the water to collect our bounty. Just as Joseph handed over the barracuda, a resident teenager approached to help but instead of wading towards the boat, he reached towards the water and scooped up a banded snake by the tail.

It looked to be about a metre long, with black and white stripes along the length of its thin body. The boy then offered it to me and said, 'You can hold it by the tail, but keep your arm out straight. They can be dangerous, but their mouths are too small to bite you.'

Fran heard the boy's laughter and greeted me by the water, as I held a barracuda in one hand and a venomous snake in the other. Joseph came to my rescue and took hold of the snake at arm's length, before returning it to the water. It swam away without a bother, towards Snake Island, just offshore.

Later that day, Fran tempted me from the hammock for the chance to go snorkelling on the nearby reef, to admire starfish and schools of parrotfish. In the last of the light, we emerged from the ocean, to enjoy a welcome blast of fresh water from the outdoor shower. Just before sunset we heard the conch once more, calling us for our evening meal. Partway through dessert, we were invited to watch a rugby tournament, due to take place on a neighbouring island the following morning. That night, lulled by the sound of waves breaking on the shore, we fell into a deep sleep.

We woke to the sound of the conch being blown. Breakfast was being served and the boat would soon be departing. The crossing took 20 minutes, with barely a ripple on the water as Joseph led us to the nearby island. This one looked larger and hillier than our one, with a village at one end and a grassy oval in the middle.

Throngs of excited children darted past the coconut trees, ignored by rugby players in search of their pitches. We settled in the shade of a tree to watch the fast-running games, joined by inquisitive children who shared our picnic of grilled fish, curried potatoes and bananas. Despite the athleticism and heroics on the playing fields, I couldn't sit still for too long. Eventually, I went in search of water, promising to return soon.

The village streets were empty as most inhabitants were lazing in the paddock, watching the tournament. I ambled past the wooden shacks, hoping to find a food kiosk or water standpipe, but after circumnavigating the village, decided to head back empty-handed. I then spotted movement as an elderly man stepped onto his porch, waved me over and called out, 'Bula.'

As I approached, he moved nearer, smiling and offering me his hand. My initial thoughts were incorrect as he looked to be middle-aged, with a healthy crop of grey hair and soft brown eyes. Feeling the need to explain my presence in the village, I rambled on about my growing thirst.

After listening for a few seconds, he smiled again. 'My name is Ratu. Please come to my house. Soon I will drink kava and I'd like you to be my guest. It is much tastier than water.'

I felt privileged to be asked and stepped onto his veranda, before finding myself in a cool hallway, decorated with family portraits hanging from plastered walls. I recognised his wife from one of the hallway pictures, when she emerged from the kitchen carrying a tray of coconut shells. She placed them on a table and diverted to the front door to greet more visitors, smiling as she passed.

Minutes later, I was standing in their living room, watching as it filled with neighbours and friends. Some came over to greet me, before finding a place to sit on a wide mat sprawled across the floor. I was the tallest adult in the room–not by much, but it was probably a first for me. I was also the thinnest. One or two players from the tournament had also made an appearance, their muddied shirts a contrast to the spotless sulus worn by many others.

Someone closed the door, blocking out most of the outside light as a hush descended on the circle of friends. Ratu had left a gap and asked me to join the group, wedging me between a middle-aged woman and a mud-stained rugby player. While sitting quietly, I let out a smile at my turn of good fortune. I didn't understand what to do next in the ritual, but decided to watch and learn.

Ratu was the first to go and all eyes were watching as he collected a coconut shell from his wife and called out, 'Bula.' It was brimming with a pale brown liquid which he drank in one go, before passing it to the next in line. He then clapped three times while calling out 'Bula,' once more.

There were three neighbours to go before my turn, giving me plenty of time to learn the etiquette. The claps were made hollow by using cupped hands, and they always finished the drink in one go. As the rugby player took his brimming cup, my mind wandered back to lager-filled nights in Tenerife. *Down in one! Down in one! Down in one!*

How quickly time flies. One minute you're knocking back beers with your mates on summer holidays, and then things change. We move on, or fall in love, grow older, or make grand plans, and suddenly those annual trips are over.

I was sucked out of my daydream as someone said, 'Hello mister, are you okay?'

The brimming shell was held ready by the rugby player and as he passed it over I called out, 'Bula,' and drank the contents in one go. I then clapped three times, remembering to say, 'Bula,' as those around me watched and smiled. I'd passed the test and settled onto the mat for a few more circuits.

The experience was like my first taste of Guinness, in my Uncle Peter's pub in the northwest of Ireland. Just like the dark stout, kava took time to appreciate. By the third offering, my initial apprehension had ebbed away, replaced by a light head and tingling lips. With each new round of drinks, my confidence grew. By now, I understood the ritual and had learned to clap in time with the others.

Lost in time, I absorbed myself in the ceremony, oblivious to the search party taking place, led by Fran. The rugby tournament had ended, and Joseph's wife was keen to return home to prepare the evening meal.

Just as the rugby player offered another drink, I heard a noise from outside. My name was being called, and by the sound of Fran's shrill voice, she was getting nearer by the second. After one last go, I stood from the mat, edged to the back of the room and waved farewell to Ratu. He came over and shook my hand, while ushering me to the front door.

I stopped by the doorway, offering my thanks, which he dismissed with a smile. While squinting in the sunlight, I stepped off his veranda, onto the dirt road, straight into Fran. She studied me for a second and then asked, 'Where have you been? Who lives in that house? We've all been searching for you. Joseph is waiting on the boat with his wife. Why do you always go missing when we're leaving somewhere?'

My face felt flushed and explanations seemed futile, so I challenged her to a race instead, arriving at the jetty in a breathless state. Joseph shook his head and smiled as I clambered on board and gave a mumbled apology.

The following morning, we took a walk around the island. Along the way, we sidestepped coconuts scattered across the ground. Some looked as though they'd only just landed, which hastened our travels along the narrow trail.

Within 15 minutes we were back at our cabin, gazing over at the hammock we were soon to leave. After breakfast, Joseph's extended family gathered by the edge of the water, singing and waving as we slipped away from the shoreline. As the boat headed across the Moturiki passage, I turned around for a final sighting of the island. All too soon, it was just a speck on the horizon.

Back on the main island, Joseph returned our handshakes with a smile and a wave. With no visitors to collect, he headed back into the ocean alone, his tiny craft soon hidden between the swells. Our worldwide travels were nearly over. Within hours, we'd be heading to Australia, welcomed as permanent residents.

Fresh off the Boat

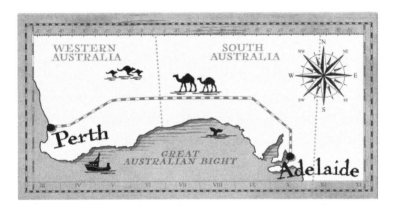

I'm not sure what we were hoping for as the baggy-eyed security officer stamped our passports in Melbourne. He'd probably grown tired of excited newcomers grinning at him at five in the morning, so just waved us through with a worn smile. I hoped an Aboriginal with a didgeridoo would be sitting in the airport lounge welcoming us with a blend of traditional sounds, but the only sign of life was a weary cleaner searching for a place to hide.

Outside the terminal, we stood in line for a taxi, huddling against each other as a cool wind tore across the street. A bright yellow cab pulled over, and we jumped inside.

'Where are you guys heading to?' the driver asked.

I took the initiative and said, 'We've just arrived, as two of the country's newest residents. Where do you reckon is a good place to visit?'

He turned and studied us with a beaming smile. 'Not more bloody Poms. Why don't you try Ningaloo Reef for a change?'

The term, *Pom*, is used on occasion by some Australians, when referring to English people. There are many theories about its inception, including the notion that English prisoners sent to Australia during colonial times became known as *Prisoners of Mother England*. Others believe the term is in reference to the pomegranate fruit, as newly arrived English people soon turn pink when exposed to the sun. Whatever the reason, it's something that the English have become accustomed to. Said in the right context, it can even be uplifting and is not something that the English seem to mind.

As for the driver's comments about visiting Ningaloo Reef, I didn't understand where he meant. It was time to buy a map of Australia! Our next stop was Adelaide, which meant a short-haul flight towards the capital city of South Australia. It was here that we met with Dave, another friend from England who had made the move down under with his family.

One look at their newly built detached home, including an outdoor pool, got us thinking about where to settle down. Over the following days, we scoured the area, searching for places to live and work. Despite the nearby hills and many wineries, along with the easy pace of life and coastal setting, we felt the urge to keep moving.

After contacting Jo and John, we hopped on a train to Western Australia. It took three days and three nights to travel across the arid interior, including the Nullarbor Plain. The name is derived from the Latin word, *nullus*, meaning *nothing*, coupled with the word *abor*, meaning *tree*.

Despite the lack of trees, there were swathes of greenery, with saltbush and ankle-high scrub carpeting the flattened landscape. As the hours passed, I gazed out of the carriage windows in search of camels. It is estimated that 100,000 of these feral animals live within the Nullarbor Plain, as descendants of those introduced in the 1840s to assist pioneer explorers with their expeditions into the interior.

With so many camels roaming the Nullarbor, I thought it would be easy to spot one. Instead, I came to realise just how vast the interior of Australia was. The barren scenery rarely changed despite the hours ticking past. Partway through the journey, an announcement by the driver stirred most passengers to life, with the realisation we were now travelling along the straightest section of rail track in the world, stretching 478 kilometres without a single curve. It was hard to believe that at the end of the track we'd be in a city of skyscrapers, close to the Indian Ocean.

The abundance of time on board and vast open spaces viewed from the windows gave us the chance to rest and assess our situation. By the time we arrived in Perth, with worn clothes and a depleted bank account, it seemed like the right time to hang up our walking boots. Ningaloo Reef would have to wait, along with all the other places in Australia we were keen to explore. We were looking forward to some home comforts, and with a sense of relief, spotted John's face amongst those waiting by the platform. As the train rolled into the city centre, I stole a last glimpse at our map. We were at the western edge of the continent, in the most isolated city in the world, without jobs or a place to call home.

John looked very different from the man we'd bumped into at the migration seminar in Sandown Park, many months earlier. The stylish jacket, designer jeans and soft leather boots had been replaced by a Billabong T-shirt, surfing shorts, and open-toed sandals. The sun had bleached his mousey hair and a designer pair of wrap-around sunglasses completed the look. He drove us along the coast towards his home, pointing out various landmarks as his four-wheel drive rumbled past million-dollar properties overlooking the wide expanse of the Indian Ocean.

The beach stretched far into the distance, with a handful of walkers dotted along the shoreline. Surprisingly, there were only a few sunbathers within view, despite the temperature gauge reading 26 Celsius. Apart from a lone kayaker playing in the waves, there was little activity on the waterfront. As John passed another stretch of golden sand, I turned the radio down and asked, 'Where is everyone? The beaches are empty, but it's the weekend and the weather looks perfect.'

His blunt reply took me by surprise. 'It's April, so this is early autumn. Those sunbathing are probably holidaymakers. It's getting too cold for most Aussies now.'

As he spoke, I remembered back to a time long ago, when in England during a summer heatwave, with temperatures in the late twenties. Like many others, I'd headed to the coast for the chance to enjoy the beach with friends. After arriving in Margate, we joined the battle to find a parking spot, along with thousands of other frazzled drivers. We then followed hordes

of tourists walking towards the beachfront, some weighed
down with deckchairs, buckets and spades.

Once on the beach, we steered our way past discarded
buckets, stepped over embracing teenagers and searched for a
vacant patch of sand. Sunburned kids queued for ice creams, as
donkeys trudged along the seafront, each with an excited tod-
dler on their back. There were very few people in the sea and
those bold enough to try, came out within minutes, shivering
as they reached for towels.

Despite the crowds, the grey sea and long queues for ice
creams, it had been a fun day, complete with a fish-and-chip
supper by the beachfront. I smiled at the memory and returned
my attention to the scene outside. As we passed alongside a
row of busy cafes, my thoughts turned to more serious matters,
including ways to replenish the finances. I was still thinking
about our depleted budget as John navigated his way through a
whisper quiet suburb and pulled onto his driveway. Jo appeared
soon after, along with their two young girls, who knocked on
the car window to say hello.

Would we ever have made it to Perth if we hadn't stopped
for a muffin and coffee during the interval at the migration
seminar? Whether it was fate, destiny or just good luck, I don't
know. But as Jo showed us to our room and then led us to the
outdoor pool, I felt as though we were in some type of dream.
We'd arrived in Australia with a rucksack each and were now
living rent-free, in a detached house near the Indian Ocean.

I was down to my last pair of decent shorts, hadn't worked
for nearly a year, and could now restart my career. I sat by the
edge of the pool, dangled my legs into the water and turned
my face towards the setting sun. The nearest country was four

hours' flight away, the nearest capital city was three days' drive away, my best mate was 14,000 kilometres away and our family expected us to return home within a few years. We were finally in Australia after years of dreaming, but I felt excited and scared at the same time. Excited about the future but scared of letting go of the past.

It felt strange to be on the world's largest island with no network of friends or family to call upon. No one in Australia knew I enjoyed long-distance walking and had once cycled 900 miles across the length of Britain, from Land's End to John O'Groats, using my brother's bike because I couldn't afford my own.

As days turned into weeks, I began reminiscing about my hometown on the other side of the world. It was the simple things that I missed. Bumping into friends at the shops, going out for beers on a Friday night, or dropping round for a cuppa with my sister. It was becoming clear that no amount of sunset walks on the nearby beach at Sorrento could subdue my senti-mental memories of life back in England.

I needed two things—a permanent job and a purpose. I'd already had an interview with a caravan manufacturer and was hoping for good news soon. My purpose came unexpectedly one hazy afternoon, when John asked me to help him collect a second-hand boat he'd just purchased. The conversation went something like this.

'I didn't know you liked boats, John.'

'I'm not sure if I do, but we're in Australia now and you've gotta live the dream. That's why we're here, isn't it?'

I smiled at his reply and asked, 'What type did you buy?'

'A big blue one.'

I shook my head in disbelief and asked, 'Do you know how to operate one?'

He gave a cheeky smile and said, 'No, not yet, but it can't be that hard.'

Four hours later, a boat called the *Sea Eagle* was parked on his driveway. It was eight metres long, painted blue and white, with twin engines and below-deck seating. We didn't know how to start the engines and had no idea what to do with all the boating equipment stowed in the hold. While Jo and the children climbed on board, John opened the owner's manual and searched for clues.

The following weekend he enrolled in an accelerated skipper's course to learn the basics of boating, which culminated in a successful man-overboard simulation in Hillary's Boat Harbour. While he studied boating regulations, I purchased two rods, a fishing magazine, an assortment of hooks, a packet of bait and a large plastic bucket. After two days of training, he passed the test and received a certificate.

That evening by his pool, we made plans to launch the boat. We decided on an early start the following morning, so we could launch the boat before the regulars showed up. As John reversed the boat down the ramp, the sun peeped over the horizon. Under a waking sky, we guided the *Sea Eagle* into the water and tied it to the mooring while starting the engines.

The launch had gone without a hitch, causing us both to smile as we inched away from land, past million-dollar yachts that had moored overnight. After we'd passed a lighting tower at the end of the groin, John turned the boat to face the gentle swell and said, 'We've finally made it to the Indian Ocean.'

We didn't venture too far from the harbour and decided to anchor close to a nearby reef. Despite all the tips and tricks in my fishing magazine, we failed to get a single bite. We were close enough to the beach to watch early morning dog walkers, and as the wind picked up, excited barks carried over the water. Soon there were jet skis in action, along with luxury yachts, heading out to sea.

With so much boat traffic, we opted for a quick blast along the coast, before heading back to the harbour in search of breakfast. As we entered the marina, the tempting smell of grilled bacon filled the air, as moored residents prepared for a day on the water.

On the main jetty, a long line of people waited to board a ferry, bound for the nearby island of Rottnest. We watched as the deckhands freewheeled bicycles up a ramp onto the bow, in readiness for departure. The marina was now wide awake, with kayakers on the water and boardwalk cafés enjoying a brisk trade.

While approaching the quayside, we realised the boat ramp was no longer quiet. With military precision, we watched two boats being launched in quick succession, their owners making the task look easy. We waited for a gap, then moored alongside the jetty. After a dash to the car park, I reversed the trailer down the slippery ramp until it lined up with the boat. The trailer had a steel cable and shackle, used for hauling boats from the water, and as John clipped it into position, I flicked the electrical switch.

Instead of the grinding of gears, we were met by silence. I tried the switch again and tugged on the wires, only to discover they'd perished with age. I then turned my attention to the manual winch, but the crank handle refused to budge. John took over, adding muscle and grunt while trying to ignore the handful of bystanders that had appeared on the scene. This time there was a satisfying squeal, as the forgotten gears came to life with each revolution.

On closer inspection, the steel cable looked frayed and worn, but held firm as the boat eased from the water. Moments later, the handle snapped in two, revealing a reddish vein of rust as it clattered to the ground! I heard giggles from a bystander and took note of the growing crowd, including dog walkers in conversation, joggers taking a break, and those who looked dressed for a day on the water and were now held up by the quayside antics.

In the panic that followed, a rash decision was made, with a plan to tie a rope from the front of the boat to the towbar of the vehicle. This would mean unhooking the trailer, so we wedged pieces of timber around each wheel. With the trailer secure, I then drove partway up the ramp and tied a rope to the towbar before throwing the other end to John, who pulled it tight while knotting it to the front of the *Sea Eagle*.

Our plan would have been perfect, except for a rogue sea breeze which pulled his boat off centre, just as I accelerated up the ramp. Instead of easing onto the rollers of the trailer, the *Sea Eagle* was dragged at an angle, buckling the metalwork while ripping a roller from its housing.

John remained calm despite the carnage and searched the crowd for a friendly face. After less than six months in the country, he was a natural at connecting with the locals. Maybe it was the bleached hair, olive complexion and easy-going manner. He held his arms wide in a gesture of submission and called out, 'Does anyone know what to do next?'

In response, one onlooker called out, 'Yes, mate. Try taking up table tennis, instead.'

He smiled at the remark and appealed for help once more. This time, there was a different reaction. One bystander unfolded his arms and tapped a friend on the shoulder to help. They ambled over, inspected the situation with an assured look, and soon had the vessel back in the water and lined up squarely. One of them requested the car keys and expertly pulled the *Sea Eagle* from the water onto the buckled trailer.

Within 15 minutes, all was calm. After promising to help repair the trailer, I treated John to a coffee as we sat in a nearby café, reliving the morning's antics. From that day on, the *Sea Eagle* gave us plenty of opportunities for adventure. Some mornings we spotted dolphins, and through trial and error we learned the art of fishing.

But minor incidents kept occurring. First, the steering failed, resulting in expensive repairs. Then the fuel system played up, causing the boat to drift onto a sandbank in the Swan River. After being towed back by sea rescue, John had the boat serviced, including an overhaul of the engines. Despite the improvements, I sensed he had less time for boating, with new business opportunities on the horizon. It seemed a perfect time for me and Fran to consider our future, including finding a place to call our own. While we searched the internet for accommodation, John suggested a farewell boating excursion.

For our final trip, we headed to Rottnest Island, 30 kilometres offshore from Perth. The stretch of deep water between the mainland and island is rarely without a boat of some type, including the ferries that transport goods and people throughout the daylight hours. We'd also studied a nautical chart, and after taking one look at the network of treacherous reefs, decided to play it safe by hiring a professional skipper.

While enquiring at the boat ramp, John got a name and number for someone that could help. The man's name was Nigel and with his help we made plans to navigate our way to the popular tourist spot.

After a quick introduction at the boat harbour, Nigel familiarised himself with all aspects of the boat, including the outboard motors, safety equipment and maintenance log. He looked to be every inch the seafarer, with his trademark tan, weathered face, flyaway hair and confident smile. To complete the look, he wore faded shorts, a collared T-shirt and seasoned plimsolls.

After giving the thumbs up, he gave the signal to untie the mooring and then let John take the helm. With barely a cloud in the sky and nothing more than a gentle breeze to stir the water, the first part of the journey proved easy enough. Soon we were chugging past the groin wall of Hillary's Boat Harbour, into open water. I stood by the railing, watching a line of anglers on the rocks, all waiting for something to bite.

Once outside the protection of the harbour wall, the boat rocked gently in the early morning swell. As our speed increased, Nigel guided John through a series of navigation channels towards open water. Two dolphins appeared soon after, surfing in our bow-wave as John throttled the engines. Throughout the crossing, they never lost a beat and purred like Cheshire cats when put to the test.

As the low-lying island crept into view, I found myself drawn to the multitude of boats and yachts, moored in the glistening waters of Thomson Bay. One was on the move and as we decreased speed, a luxury yacht passed close by, its passengers lounging on a wide deck, drinks in hand while smiling down at us.

Minutes later, we were idling at a snail's pace and Nigel was leaning over the side to secure us to an anchor point. As I gazed into the crystal-clear water, a school of silvery baitfish darted past, followed by a graceful stingray. After tethering the boat, we stepped barefoot into the warm, waist-deep water and headed across the sandy bottom towards a grassy bank.

Each of us carried a daypack on our backs, filled with footwear, water bottles, sunscreen and a few dollars. After stepping ashore, Nigel pointed towards a sandstone building at the end of a treelined walkway. 'I need to head to the visitor's centre to sort out the mooring fee. The ferry from Freo is about to dock, so I want to get ahead of the pack. While I'm gone, try to see if you can spot any quokkas.'

With that, he strolled barefoot towards the visitor's centre. After watching him go, I turned to John and asked, 'Where's Freo and what's a quokka?'

He was sitting on the grass, rummaging through his bag, and looked up at me with a smile. 'Freo is the nickname for the port of Fremantle. You should know by now that Australians love to shorten every name and place.'

Just then I heard the rumble of motors and turned to watch as a large catamaran came into dock by the quayside. There were dozens of bicycles on the upper deck, and as soon as they'd secured the ship, the crew began unloading them. The jetty was soon milling with people of all shapes and sizes, including excited children, kept from the edge by a sturdy railing. While some passengers waited for their bikes to be wheeled off, others set off towards the visitor's centre, to prepare for their stay on the island.

As we made our way to the quayside, John pointed towards a colourful billboard, welcoming us to Rottnest. The image depicted a map of the island, with symbols to show the best places to swim, snorkel, fish or enjoy refreshments. The perimeter of the island looked to have dozens of intimate coves of all shapes and sizes. Some were close to Thomson Bay, but there were many others on the far side of the island, which looked ideal for those seeking a castaway experience.

The map also highlighted bus stops in certain areas around the island, for those wanting to take advantage of the hop-on, hop-off, service. There was also a picture of a small, furry creature, with a shiny black nose and jolly looking face. 'That's a quokka,' John explained.

As I studied the image, he said, 'Don't spend too long looking at the photo, as you'll see one in real life soon enough. They're marsupials, just like kangaroos, but far smaller and cuter.'

I didn't see any cute and cuddly creatures nearby, but spotted a man in his fifties, bounding out of the visitor's centre towards us. As Nigel approached, he called out, 'That was a close one. There are heaps of people queuing for room keys. This place seems to get busier every year.'

John then took the initiative and said, 'Well, I don't know about you two, but I'm ready for breakfast and have a great little place in mind.'

As he led the way, Nigel gave me a running commentary about the island. 'There are heaps of chalets to choose from, but if you want one during Christmas, you need to book well ahead. They used to be run down, but I've heard they're in better shape these days. Most are a stone's throw from the Indian Ocean, and the kids love the place as there are no cars allowed, apart from those owned by the authorities.'

'How big is the police force?' I asked.

'I've no idea. In fact, I've hardly ever seen anyone in uniform. I guess the place kicks off at New Year, like the rest of the country, so maybe they get busy then.'

We were passing a row of detached chalets and I stopped to study the nearest one, which had a paved veranda outside the front door. There was also a low-lying wall and a garden gate, held closed by a latch. Nigel rattled the gate and said, 'It's mainly to keep the quokkas out as they are mischievous creatures.'

As I searched for quokkas in the street, he explained about the accommodation on offer throughout the island. 'Most units and chalets have got the basics, including a barbeque, kitchen, shower, toilet and TV area.'

For those wanting luxury, he recommended Rottnest Lodge, with its spa, pool and yoga retreat, or Hotel Rottnest for the ocean-view suites, beachside bar and restaurant. I'd only been on the island a matter of minutes and was already transfixed with the peace and tranquillity. There were no high-rise buildings to obscure the ocean views or any cars to watch out for on the winding roads.

As we approached the café, four children cycled into view, each one wearing a mandatory helmet. Two of them were holding fishing rods, with plastic buckets swinging from their handlebars. The others were dressed for the beach, with snorkels, fins and masks protruding from mesh backpacks, as they rode past, four abreast, while giggling and chatting.

After they'd gone, Nigel pointed out some local landmarks. 'Over there is the main precinct which has a bakery and a few shops. You'll enjoy the pies and the coffee is perfect. The lighthouse is a ten-minute cycle ride away, with an amazing little cove below it. The snorkelling is awesome, with heaps of fish. Just inland, you'll find a whitewashed cottage that used to be the home of an ex-convict...'

While he continued speaking, my mind wandered off. This was the kind of place I'd been yearning to find since arriving in Perth and I couldn't wait to tell Fran all about it. By now, we were standing outside the café and John was studying a menu. With a promise to meet up soon, I went in search of a last-minute photo opportunity.

While walking towards a stretch of dazzling sand, I spotted movement by a tree. I stopped to grab my camera as a small, furry creature hopped into view. It looked to be the size of a tomcat, with thick, greyish-brown hair and a shiny black nose. I'd just found my first quokka!

It turned its back on me and started foraging amongst fallen leaves. I edged closer, then dropped to my knees, just as it turned to face me. To my surprise and delight, it hopped a little nearer. I then lay on my stomach, so I could study its happy little face.

As I lay still, a cyclist went past, smiling at my attempts to get up close with the quokka. The next person who came along wore a yellow T-shirt and dark shorts. She looked to be in her fifties and wore a nylon lanyard around her neck, which held an

ID badge. She stopped to smile as I jumped to my feet. 'It looks like you're trying to make friends with a quokka,' she said.

I didn't know if I was in trouble or not, so stood sheepishly as the quokka hopped nearer and sniffed my bare feet. The woman grinned and said, 'Hi there, I'm Janet. I'm one of the volunteers on the island. You haven't done anything wrong, but it's worth knowing they are a protected species. Thankfully, everyone falls in love with them and they have a carefree life on the island, as there are no natural predators and very few vehicles to worry about.'

She then dropped to her knees to study the chirpy-looking creature. 'Mind you, it's hard to get away from them sometimes. They're the friendliest animals in the world I reckon, and can be very mischievous. We find them in many places and they appear at the pub most evenings, even if there is live music playing.'

She then explained how the island got its name. In 1696, a Dutch sailor and explorer named Willem de Vlamingh thought the quokkas were enormous rats, instead of native marsupials. He named it *Rats Nest Island*, or in Dutch, *Rottenest Island*. Somewhere down the line, the letter 'e' was dropped, and today we know it as Rottnest. The local Aboriginal people also have a name for the island, dating back much further than the 1600s. The Whadjuk Nyoongar know it as *Wadjemup*, which means 'the land across the sea where the spirits are.'

Although keen to listen further, the sight of John at the café entrance, holding aloft a menu, told me I had to go. Twenty minutes later I was seated on the veranda with John and Nigel, tucking into a Spanish omelette. From our vantage point, we watched people at play on their boats and could hear children's laughter as they splashed in the shallows. For a fleeting moment, I considered running across the sand to take a swim.

Instead, I lazed in my seat, sipped freshly squeezed orange juice and watched a mother quokka with her joey. The youngster showed little fear as it hopped under our table, followed closely by its mother. They rummaged for a while between our legs, then found a gap in the railings and hopped towards nearby bushes.

We also needed to be on the move, as Nigel had a lunchtime appointment in Perth. Just as we left the café, a group of young women walked past, chatting away in a language I didn't understand. One of them pulled out a camera and as the others stood together, I offered to take a photo of them all.

With ease, the nearest girl switched to fluent English while handing me her camera. 'That's very kind, thank you.'

After taking a quick snap, I soon learned they were students from Singapore and had booked a night on the island. They were having trouble reading the tourist map and were trying to find their chalet. They seemed to be forever giggling as I pointed out where they were and tried explaining the best way to their accommodation.

Just as I'd figured out a shortcut, one woman pointed towards a patch of grass and called out, 'Quokka. A quokka. Oh, so cute.'

They left me standing with their map and made a dash for the quokka. I placed the pamphlet on a nearby bench and watched from afar as they lay close to the placid creature, each holding a phone aloft to capture a selfie. The quokka obliged and hopped between them all, resulting in more fits of giggles.

On our return to the mainland, John announced an end to his ocean-faring days. The *Sea Eagle* was snapped up soon after, by a man who looked very similar to Nigel. With the boat gone and John making other grand plans, it seemed that change was in the air. Since our arrival in Perth, Jo and John had given us a significant head start, but we needed to find our own way. After fond farewells, we promised to stay in touch and moved into a rental unit, just 200 metres away!

Lemon scented gum trees surrounded the complex, their canopies offering welcome shade as we sat each morning, watching rainbow lorikeets darting from tree to tree, waking the neighbourhood with their screeches and squawks. They were hard to ignore, not only for their mischievous treetop antics but also their colourful plumage of red, violet blue, and woodland green.

After a trip to the local library for the lend of a book, I discovered the birds were an introduced species, either by accident or after being released. From a small number in the 1960s, they've continued to flourish in the Perth region, causing damage to plants and crops. Although beautiful to watch, they made me consider I was also a newcomer to the region, hoping to spread my wings and make a home with Fran.

In a country as popular as Australia, there is always change, as new arrivals look to settle. Some blend in, others make a fuss and cause a ruffle. Only time would tell where we'd find a permanent place to nest.

Where The Streets Have No Name

"Do not cut down the tree that gives you shade."
– Arabian Proverb

A few weeks after moving into the unit, I began work in a city centre café, helping to serve coffee and toasties to early morning commuters. Fran also secured a part-time job, as a teacher's aide in a primary school. I continued searching for similar roles to the one I'd enjoyed in England although I couldn't commit to returning to a fast-paced production environment, focused on targets and efficiency!

After months of travel, I wanted to ease into working life, with less responsibility and more time to enjoy the sights and sounds of Australia. Our packs were already gathering dust in the garage and our walking boots had not been worn since we'd bounded across the hills of Tasmania. During moments of nostalgia, I'd pause by our redundant rucksacks, remembering times when they'd been hauled across the Inca Trail or used as backrests after a long day on the open road.

Since then, our lives had transformed. Instead of meandering across the globe on a midlife adventure, we were now looking to make roots in a new country. Soon, we'd need a permanent home and secure jobs, along with the task of making connections in the community, either through sport or volunteering. Ideally, we'd have had months to settle into our new way of life, including our comfy rental just a few hundred metres from the beach.

Unfortunately, the housing market was waking after years of hibernation, causing a stir in the media. Although I tried hiding from the headlines, the hysteria became too loud to ignore. Land shortages and suburban hotspots became popular topics on radio and TV shows, with experts predicting significant price rises in the foreseeable future. The talk of a land shortage surprised me, considering the vastness of Western Australia and sparse population, with an estimated density of 0.9 people per square kilometre.

Compared to the busy streets of the UK, with 277 people per square kilometre, the numbers for Western Australia may seem low, until you realise that many parts of the state are inhospitable, especially in the north and west, away from the coastline.

Further investigation revealed that an influx of skilled workers from interstate and overseas was adding to the demand for Perth housing. New developments were required, and most homebuyers wanted to be close to the Indian Ocean, resulting in large tracts of bushland to the north of the city being planned as satellite communities.

As the weather cooled, reports continued about Perth being on the cusp of a property boom. This prompted me to think back to my first foray into the property market, with the purchase of a century-old, two-bedroom terraced house in my hometown in England. It had been a poorly timed decision, with interest rates set to soar. Within a few years, the property halved in value while the repayments doubled.

I'd been spooked before and now felt scared of making the same mistake, even though I was in a different country, in a thriving city fuelled by demand from China for iron ore. One of our initial reasons for moving to Perth had been the moderate property prices compared to other parts of Australia. Now, it seemed, we needed to act quickly, or risk being left behind.

Fran took control one Saturday, prompted by bold headlines in the newspaper of imminent price hikes for property and land. 'Ali, there's a land sale on this morning. Before heading to the markets, we could take a drive north to see what's available.'

This time I paid heed to the newspaper, wondering if there was nothing else to report in Perth, apart from rising property prices. The supplement was filled with colourful advertisements promoting new subdivisions on the outskirts of the city, with appealing names like Eagles Landing, Stockman's Retreat and Ocean Gardens. Site works were already under way for manicured parks, shopping centres, schools and playgrounds, all within reach of the Indian Ocean. It all seemed too good to be true and it was time to investigate.

Breakfast was abandoned in our haste for the door, with a swift detour for drive-through coffee and muffins. We drove north under clear skies until the freeway ended, forcing us onto a recently built carriageway. The land on either side had once been pristine bushland, but the trees, birds and animals were now replaced by empty streets and half-built houses. The road was busier than I'd imagined, with a steady stream of cars and trucks going both ways, loaded with people or building supplies.

Twenty minutes later we spotted pockets of bushland, as the road narrowed to a single lane. Fluttering flags and advertising boards lined the last stretch of tarmac, depicting happy families at play on a beach. Further ahead, the road ended, with a gravelled car park etched into the bush, signalling the furthest outpost of Perth.

The bays were filling fast and as we squeezed into a spot, I noticed a portable cabin close by, with the words *Land Sale* displayed across the front. To our left stood the most northerly street in Perth, without a single resident. Each show home looked immaculate, with manicured gardens and rows of newly planted saplings dotted across a verge of velvet green, being treated to a watering from automatic sprinklers. Each garden had a placard outside, revealing the name of the builder ready to be signed up to construct a dream home.

While studying the row of show homes, I thought back to an article in the paper, giving sound advice. *Get your block first, then find a house design to match your taste and budget.* With this in mind, we strolled towards the sales office, alongside a family of four that had bounded out of a nearby car. I held the cabin door open as the man and wife dashed inside, ushering their teenage children through while calling out a thank you.

Inside, potential buyers flicked through the listings on offer while standing around a papier-mâché layout that stood centre stage, representing the developer's vision. There was an air of anticipation, as those inside spoke in hushed voices while mulling over the information. As Fran hunted for a brochure, I studied the smorgasbord of potential buyers, listening to familiar accents from parts of Great Britain and Ireland, along with those from South Africa. I even heard Australians and Kiwis in the mix!

Above the entrance door, a bright poster read: *Stage 9 selling fast. Stage 10 land release in three months.*

I turned to Fran and whispered, 'Let's forget about visiting the markets. We need to buy some land and the time to do it is today.'

Her eyes widened. 'Ali, we need to think about this.'

But I was caught up in the moment and persisted. 'Look around. This is the 1889 Oklahoma land rush all over again and I'm not waiting until the only available plot is a patch of parched earth, deep in Indian country.'

She studied me quizzically. 'What are you on about? Have you been watching cowboy films again?'

In reply, I pointed to the entrance. 'Look at the faces of that couple by the doorway. Their eyes bulged as soon as they walked in and saw the number of people inside. Everybody here is intent on buying a piece of land. No-one is window shopping anymore, as there's no time to wait and they're all spooked. I'm telling you, by this afternoon all these blocks will be gone, and the next stage will rise by tens of thousands.'

In response, she lowered her voice and stepped closer. 'Since when have you been a property expert?'

'Never, and my track record shows that I've only ever bought at the peak. If we buy today, for once in my life I'll be ahead!'

She smiled softly and said, 'You're being very dramatic, but let's have a look around.'

While Fran studied her brochure, I nudged through the crowd towards the papier mâché model to learn more about the planned estate. A couple in their mid-twenties joined me soon after, their voices barely audible over the hum of the air conditioner. The man was casually dressed, wearing football shorts and a matching blue and gold T-shirt emblazoned with the words, *West Coast Eagles Football Club.*

I couldn't help but listen, hoping to pick up a few tips about buying land. They sounded Australian and the man had a clear plan as he lowered his voice to talk with his partner. 'Block 201 is perfect. It has a north facing back garden where the pool can go, and we can fit an alfresco on the west side to catch any sea breeze.'

As they headed to the front desk, I moved away and pulled Fran to one side. 'Block 201 is about to go. It's all about having your back garden facing north for the sunshine and thinking about westerly breezes.'

I then took a breath and asked the decisive question. 'Fran, what do you think? Should we give it a go?'

In reply, she gave a mischievous smile and said, 'Yes, let's do it. I'll join the queue while you get to work.'

She was soon third in line to fill in a registration slip, which would take less than a minute per person. All she needed was the number of the block we wanted to purchase. With three minutes to locate our dream block, I set to work, as the queue behind her continued to grow. I recognised the couple at the front, as the ones after block 201, and turned my attention to the papier-mâché layout. Block 202 looked favourable, which meant we'd be their neighbours in the months ahead!

Maybe they'd let us use their pool and we could enjoy cold beers together on their alfresco while discussing the technicalities and origins of Australian Football. With the numbers 202 scribbled on my hand, I made my way towards Fran, but mid-stride a sales representative hushed the room. 'Please be aware that blocks 201, 202 and 209 are now on hold.'

Well, there went the new neighbours and the chance to learn about the footy! Fran raised her hands in confusion as I dashed back to the papier-mâché model, my heart racing while weighing up the remaining options, including a corner block with an eastern-facing garden or a smaller block closer to the beach.

Fran was now at the front of the queue and called out to me, eager for help! After one last look at the layout, I made a once-in-a-lifetime decision, memorised the number of the chosen block, and strolled past the queue of hopeful punters standing behind Fran. Moments later, we put a deposit down for a corner block with an east facing rear garden.

'Great choice,' cooed the sales rep. 'I've always loved block 214.'

A young woman standing behind me overheard the rep and let out a sigh, before stomping towards the papier-mâché model. I felt a pang of guilt, knowing we'd signed for the block she wanted, and watched as she dialled a friend to vent her fury.

The customer rep handed over a glossy map of the new subdivision and circled our block in red ink, to help us locate it. We walked past the growing queue and with a mixed feeling of excitement and trepidation, stepped into bright sunshine, in search of a wooden peg somewhere in the nameless streets.

Once clear of the car park and flags, it was obvious there was little in the way of infrastructure. The entire area was morphing from vision into reality, and most bushland had been stripped bare. The result was a featureless terrain of yellow sand interwoven with black tarmac. Most developers, it seemed, went in for the shock and awe tactic of levelling the land to make for easy building. A few patches of bush had been spared the axe, for use as parkland, which sat alongside an artificial lake the size of a football field. The strip of land overlooking the lake had been dissected into narrow blocks, all with sold signs.

Eyes peeled, we took a drive along the empty streets, counting out loud each block number, until we reached a patch of sand marked as 214. After parking on our block, I studied the neighbourhood. We were surrounded by a gently sloping paddock of cleared land, devoid of buildings. Each parcel of land had a boundary wall standing a metre high and many blocks within view had sold signs hammered into the earth.

According to the map, our block was about a kilometre from the Indian Ocean, and I suddenly felt excited at the prospect of an ocean view. 'Get on my shoulders, Fran. You might see the waves.'

She was keen to try, and after clambering on, got the chance to look west in search of the ocean. 'Oh, yes, I think I can see a boat on the horizon.'

After she'd returned safely back to earth, we stood together and studied the map. Although there was a slim chance of an ocean view from a second storey, the price of such a house was above our budget. Land prices increased with each step nearer to the beach and we couldn't afford to get any closer. Now I understood why some buyers chose to purchase by the manicured lake, with water views at a reduced cost. The beachside homes were going to be million-dollar properties, and many would be two-storey due to the narrow size of the blocks.

We sat on the boundary wall, finished the last of our water and waited for the breeze to cool us down. With no houses nearby, we could see far across the levelled ground and watched as the new owners of block 201 measured their backyard. The guy was taking giant steps across the sand, checking where their pool would go. It was then that I had a thought. 'Fran, what can you hear?'

She looked across at me. 'Nothing much, just a bulldozer in action and that man calling numbers out to his wife.'

'Anything else?'

'What are you on about?'

'There's no sound of wildlife. No birds singing, kangaroos hopping or parrots squawking. Just thousands of ants marching across the sand, and they don't make a sound.'

We studied the sky and watched a flock of rose-breasted cockatoos fly overhead, but none stopped to rest. Why would they? There was nothing to eat and nowhere to roost. I understood that the development would eventually become established, and new homeowners would lay manicured lawns with neat borders. Many residents would introduce vegetable plots and plant seedlings, but trees would take years to grow tall.

Somehow, the buzz of purchasing our own land and finding a master builder to create a dream home no longer seemed so appealing. I remembered back to my wedding speech–with dreams about living in the countryside with Fran, having free-range chickens and maybe even a Vietnamese potbellied pig. The nearest chicken to this block would be Kentucky fried in the new fast-food takeaway being built in the master planned shopping centre.

As we sat together, lost in thought, Fran turned to me and said, 'Why don't we try looking in an older suburb, for an established house next to parkland?'

It was clear that the Oklahoma land rush was not meant for us, although it had been an eventful morning. After a trip to the office to hand back our block, we drove along the empty streets one more time, spotting the couple who'd purchased block 201. The man was too busy pacing his west-facing alfresco to look up.

A few months later, I strolled to our local deli to collect the Saturday paper. Although winter, the sun warmed my face as I stopped to admire a flock of noisy parrots nestled in nearby trees. Back at home I sat on the veranda of our twenty-year-old-property while Fran made tea and toast. We then sat together and read the headline, thinking back to all those we'd met at the sales office during our search for vacant land.

Campers in a two-week queue for the next land release as prices rise by twenty percent.

Instead of moving to a new development we'd opted to live in an older suburb and were pleased to find that our leafy neighbourhood contained a cosmopolitan mix. The majority were Australians (both white and indigenous), with a complement of Europeans, South Africans, and Asians. The lawns in our street were well kept, the ocean was only a ten-minute drive away, and the local children were playful and polite. Fran was blooming in the early stages of pregnancy, and we'd found our first Australian home.

Here for You

"Every child is an artist. The problem is how to remain an artist once he grows up."
– Pablo Picasso

By the height of summer, Fran was in full bloom. Newfound friends rallied to help as we prepared for the birth, and in the New Year a welcome call came from England. Alice was on her way, to offer support during the final stages. The last time I'd seen my sister had been during our travels across Sydney, Melbourne and Tasmania.

She stayed with us in Perth for three weeks, helping day and night, before heading home to England. In response, I wrote a poem about my travels with Fran and the special relationship she had with Alice.

*

Fran, we once lived as nomads,
    Travelling the world together,
    From Mount Kilimanjaro to the Andes.
    In places we ran for our lives,
    From wild creatures and underground explosions.
    We also found solitude and adventure,
    In the jungles of Ecuador and wilds of Namibia.
    In the most isolated city in the world,
    You whispered,
    I'm pregnant.

But we have no family nearby,
And you have so many questions,
About birth plans, pregnancy and childcare.
Then a call comes from England,
And everything will be fine,
Alice is on her way.
Mary Poppins, I think, as she waltzes through customs,
Dressed for action,
With gifts, goodies, and a sisterly hug.
Under crimson skies, you both walk barefoot,
Like best friends,
Along golden beaches.
Each evening, over drinks and nibbles,
A warm breeze to stir the leaves,
Alice shares stories and gives gentle advice,
About being a new mum,
Including the joys, emotions and challenges.
Three weeks later, Alice prepares to head home,
She wants to stay longer, but has run out of time,
But first, there is a gift;
Steve Martin is funny in *Parenthood*, she says.
In the last weeks, Fran's belly swells,
Prompting wild stares from strangers,
It won't be long now.
We were laughing out loud,
While watching Steve Martin on screen,
Followed by silence,
As Fran's waters broke.
Remote in hand, movie paused,
I searched frantically,

For the overnight bag,
While Fran stayed calm,
And followed the birth plan,
Created weeks before, with Alice.
With a hearty cry,
Noah James came into our world,
A new Australian, born to migrants.
I returned to an empty house,
To be greeted by Steve Martin,
Flickering on the TV,
His tired smile,
Welcoming me to Parenthood.

Go Wild in the Country

"Not all classrooms have four walls."
– Unknown

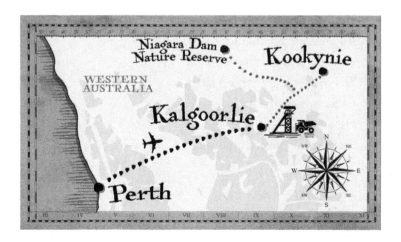

My next adventure in Australia was triggered by a weekend phone call from England, lasting only a few minutes. After switching off the phone, I found Fran in the kitchen and broke the news. 'We need to get the spare room ready again.'

'That sounds exciting. Who is it this time?'

'Alan and Sam are coming over for Christmas. And Blake, of course.'

Fran took the news with a beaming smile before heading towards a wall calendar, pen in hand to make notes. 'We'd better finish the pool decking and get the bar fridge stocked up.'

Getting visitors from England was becoming a common trend each summer, as family and friends escaped the cold and rain in the UK and celebrated Christmas in the sunshine. Alan and Sam were good friends, and their son, Blake, was already looking forward to a planned trip to Rottnest Island. I'd worked with Alan for many years at Vauxhall Motors in Luton until the day the factory gates closed forever.

A decade earlier, we'd lived under the same roof, with Alan as the easy-going landlord, while I paid my way with weekly rent and the occasional cooked meal. Those carefree days were now distant memories, but Sam loved Alan's adventurous streak and their relationship had flourished from the moment they'd met in Gretna Green, Scotland. At the time I'd been on a 13-day, 900-mile cycle ride across Britain with Alan and another good friend, Nick. The impromptu meeting at Gretna Green had changed the lives of Alan and Sam, who subsequently married a year later.

Just before our telephone conversation finished, Alan confirmed that his spirit of adventure remained strong. 'Ali, do you reckon you could organise a road trip for the both of us, for three or four days? You know, something different. Maybe we could see a bit of the real Australia. What do you think?'

I was eager to please and replied in an instant. 'That sounds like a bit of a challenge. I'll get back to you soon.'

After putting down the phone, I thought back to his comment about the real Australia. It seemed to me that the *real* Australia was hard to grasp. Many Australian travel websites were filled with images of kangaroos lazing on golden beaches, or lonely outback roads, carving their way through the harsh red centre. Others mentioned little-known surfing spots or gave mouth-watering lists of the best culinary experiences in each state. With so much variety on offer, I needed to focus.

That evening, as I lazed by the pool reading the weekend newspaper, a mid-page article caught my eye. It was about an historic event in 1962, when many residents of Perth decided to turn their lights on so that John Glenn, the first American to orbit the earth, could locate the city during his historic space flight. The illuminations were such a success that Perth became known around the world as The City of Light.

After reading the article, I turned off the outside lamp and stared towards space. Perth had grown since that pivotal space flight, and despite the ambient light of night-time suburbia, I could just make out the faint swirl of a million stars or more, flickering above the most isolated city in the world.

I suddenly felt alone and far away from family. I closed my eyes and thought once more of my childhood in England and those lazy summer days, with Mum sitting on the front porch while I played football in the street with friends. Since moving to Australia, each call from family and friends triggered another yearning to return. Although it was wrong to do so, I kept comparing Australia with England. Conversations I had with other migrants from the UK often went something like this:

Me: 'Do you miss England?'

Them: *'I miss my family and friends but not the traffic jams and grey skies.'*

Me: 'What about the English countryside?'

Them*: 'I miss the greenery, the hills and the village pubs. But I live near the beach and love the weather.'*

Maybe it was just me. I still missed the grittiness and bustle of London, the rolling hills and steep crags of the Lake District, the historic theatres of Covent Garden, and the notion I could get a train from London in the morning and arrive in Paris for an early lunch. Although I'd never taken the Eurostar for a Parisian day trip, I was fascinated by the apparent ease with which it was possible.

There is only one way out of Western Australia by train, on the Indian Pacific, heading east across the vast interior where it reaches Sydney after four days. It seemed to me that most residents of Perth, established and newly arrived, were happy with their isolation as long as the sun was shining. Empty beaches, feisty waves, fresh coffee, hot summers, traffic lights, traffic jams, fast food, new shopping malls, and sprawling suburbs were the type of Australian lifestyle I kept experiencing.

Since our global travels, I still craved flea markets, the smell of spices on the trade winds and colourful characters from faraway places. Even the Australians I'd met since arriving in Perth seemed tame. Not that I expected Crocodile Dundee to serve me coffee at the local café each weekend, but where were all the charismatic locals promised in the brochures?

When I'd arrived in Perth with Fran, my rucksack had contained a sleeping bag, camping equipment and road-weary clothes, along with a journal filled with scribbles and maps that I planned to turn into a travel story one day. During our time in South America and Africa, we'd been charged by rhinos, stalked by lions and had to run from danger whilst deep underground in a Bolivian mine. Now, the only excitement seemed to be the early morning scramble to avoid the morning rush hour. The call from Alan had come at the right time.

The following Sunday, I took a morning stroll with Fran and Noah along a coastal footpath. Joggers were doing their thing and at a beachside café a group of red-faced cyclists were dismounting, to queue for coffee. As Noah snoozed in his pusher, I sat with Fran around a nearby table, listening to how far they'd travelled as they compared times and discussed future cycling events.

While I sipped my coffee, Fran gestured towards the cyclists. 'When Alan comes over, just remember that he loves doing things unique to each location he visits. While you were cycling from Land's End to John O'Groats with him and Nick, didn't he insist on sampling local produce in each new region?'

Her question conjured up fond memories of my cycling escapades across Britain many years earlier. During our time in Cornwall, Alan sampled a Cornish pasty from a village bakery, and after crossing the border into Devon, enjoyed a riverside stop for cream teas. By the time we got to Somerset, he was in the mood for a refreshing pint of cider or two. The tradition continued as we travelled across the Highlands of Scotland, where he enjoyed a wee dram of locally distilled whisky in each bar in Aviemore, then cycled 70 miles the following morning with a thumping headache. While on holiday with him on the west coast of Ireland, he'd switched to Guinness for the week and enjoyed talking to every fisherman, sheep farmer and musician who came into my uncle's pub.

Alan was a great man to have travelling with you. He embraced each location, craved local knowledge and didn't mind getting his hands dirty. I wanted to find an excursion or activity that would leave a lasting impression–something unique to Australia. Perth is not renowned for being an adventure capital, and after listening to Fran's advice, I sensed the answer lay beyond the manicured lawns and new housing estates.

That evening as we sat by the pool, I asked her, 'Can you see the Southern Cross when you gaze at the stars?'

She put down her wine and stared into space. After a few seconds she said, 'No, I don't think I can. It's too hard with all the streetlights.'

'Exactly,' I agreed. 'If Alan wants a real adventure, then I'll take him away from the city and into the bush. I'm going to track down an Aboriginal guide. Instead of five-star comfort, we'll sleep under the stars each night.'

She picked up her wineglass and held it high. 'There you go. I always knew you'd crack the problem.'

With the plan taking shape, I felt the adrenalin rush once more, at the thought of a new adventure. Over the next few days, I called tourist information centres throughout Australia, to request the names of local Aboriginal guides. One such call went like this:

'Alice Springs Information Centre, how may I help?'

'Hi, my name's Alistair and I'm after information on hiring an Aboriginal guide.'

'I'm sorry, but we don't have anything to hire. This is an information centre. Would you like to book a ticket for the Aboriginal Explorer?'

'What's the Aboriginal Explorer?'

'It's popular with some of our overseas visitors. We run a half-day tour from Alice Springs into the bush to learn about the native plants and animals. At the end of the tour, we drive to Anzac Hill to enjoy a magical sunset. Afterwards, you can watch Aboriginals perform a traditional ceremony in a local hotel and they also play the didgeridoo. The minibus is air-conditioned, and a three-course dinner is included.'

It sounded too tame for Alan, so I changed tack and asked another question. 'Is there anything, you know, more authentic? This might sound funny, but I'm in search of the *real* Australia.'

Before she could reply, the words spilled out as I rushed to explain my thoughts. 'I don't want air-conditioned comfort. I want an Aboriginal guide to take a friend and me on an adventure, to teach us to hunt and share stories about the Dreamtime. Each evening we'll camp under the stars, then fall asleep while gazing at the Milky Way.'

For a few seconds, there was an awkward silence. Then she lowered her voice. 'I think I know what you mean, but we don't get many calls about that type of thing. Please hold and I'll ask around the office.'

She must have covered the phone with her hand, as all I could hear was a hushed voice while she spoke with colleagues. 'I've got this guy on the line. He's English, I think. He wants to learn about bush skills and is after an Aboriginal guide. Does anyone do this? He seems genuine enough.'

I soon heard her voice again, crisp and clear. 'Hello, and thanks for holding. I know this sounds crazy, but no one seems to do this anymore. I'm really sorry.'

Although she seemed to have empathy for my predicament, I couldn't hold back my frustration. 'Are you telling me there is not one Aboriginal guide that can take me on a walka-bout?'

'Well, there might be a few, but we rarely get calls for that type of request. Most people want a morning tour, followed by lunch, and then they head back to their accommodation to relax. I can book you onto one of those if you like and have availability for tomorrow, but somehow I don't think it's for you and your friend.'

I thanked the woman and hung up, then tried putting the conversation into context. In Kenya, you can walk with Maasai tribes across their pastoral lands, and in Peru you can experience life in a remote jungle village. But in Australia, the only indigenous activity I could find was watching tribal ceremonies taking place in hotel lobbies. I knew there would be much more on offer and delved deeper.

After typing 'Adventure Australia' into the Google search engine, the screen was filled with multiple options. I recognised most of the locations but didn't have the time and budget to snorkel on the Great Barrier Reef or join an overland tour from Sydney to Fraser Island. I was after somewhere more local and refined the search to, 'Adventure Western Australia Aboriginal Guide.'

The results were disappointing, unless I chose a day trip from Perth to an area known as the Pinnacles, for a walk in the desert alongside thousands of limestone pillars, some reaching three metres high. Billy Connolly, the famous Scottish comedian, once toured Australia as part of a TV travel series. While at the Pinnacles, he ran naked alongside the formations, just as the sun set behind him. Although they were worthy of a visit, I felt a day trip wouldn't quench Alan's thirst for adventure and continued to search.

Only the desperate keep scrolling through page after page on Google, and by this stage I fitted this category perfectly. It was on page 12 that I found a promising link. It took me to a basic web page that read, *Learn about Aboriginal people, Aboriginal culture, bush tucker and the Dreamtime. Tours start and finish in Kalgoorlie.*

The rest of the article gave me a name and number and within seconds I was on the phone! It answered on the fifth ring, and the voice at the other end sounded deep and relaxed. 'Hello, who is speaking, please?'

'Hi, my name is Alistair. I've just seen your article on the web about bush tucker tours and would like to talk with Geoff about going—'

'Where do you want to go?'

'Are you Geoff?'

'Yes, of course I am. You just called my number. What type of experience are you after?'

'I don't know, really. My friend is coming over from England, and we'd like an Aboriginal adventure together. After lots of searching, I found your name on Google.'

There was a moment of silence, and then he asked, 'When do you want to go?'

'How about the eighteenth of December, for three nights?'

'That should be okay, but you'll both need to realise that it will be getting hot by then. I'll take you into the bush, no worries. Maybe we'll talk about the Dreamtime and I'll teach you how to find bush tucker. Does that sound like the type of thing you're after?'

I gripped the phone, feeling the excitement rising in my voice. 'That's great, Geoff. What about payment and where to meet?'

'I won't charge you much. Just call me when you arrive. Bring a sleeping bag, a camping knife and a torch and make sure you wear old clothes. What's your friend's name?'

'Alan.'

'He's English, hey, like you. Has he been to the bush before?'

'No, like I said—'

'Does he eat kangaroo?'

'Don't worry about Alan, as he'll eat anything. Geoff, can I just confirm that—'

I was cut off as he called out, 'I gotta go. Call me when you're in Kalgoorlie.'

As I put down the phone, I felt the adrenalin rising. We'd be taking an excursion into what visitors call *The Outback* and Australians call *The Bush*. This is their name that symbolises the interior and describes many landscapes, from desert to savannah. It is a vast semi-desert, typified by extremes, where searing daytime temperatures can plunge as darkness descends.

Each evening the ancient landscape is bathed in red as the setting sun ignites the ochre embedded into the earth and rock, captivating all those who venture into the heartland. It is an unforgiving environment, sparsely populated by farmers, pastoralists, prospectors, and Aboriginal townships. Thriving communities do exist in the heat and dust. Their wealth comes from deep underground and one of the most famous outback cities is Kalgoorlie, located in south-central, Western Australia.

Kalgoorlie owes its existence to an Irish prospector called Paddy Hannan, who discovered 100 ounces of gold near Mt Charlotte in 1893. Within days of staking his claim, the surrounding bushland was swamped with hundreds of prospectors, as gold fever spread across Western Australia. By 1903 there were 49 operating mines within an area that became known as the Golden Mile, because of the abundance of precious metal found deep below.

By the 1980s, many of the original leases had become too dangerous or uneconomical to mine, which prompted an idea by a flamboyant businessman called Alan Bond, to purchase each lease and combine them into a vast, open cut mine, managed by a single company. Although unable to achieve his vision, other investors stepped in, resulting in substantial changes across the mining sector in Kalgoorlie. Apart from the nearby workings at Mt Charlotte, underground mining was phased out, in favour of digging up every piece of dirt and rock to check for gold.

Known as the Super Pit, the man-made hole is so large that it can be seen from space. The mining company that owns the Super Pit runs its operations 24 hours per day, seven days a week. During this time, it hauls thousands of tonnes of earth from the pit floor to the crushers and harvests about 800,000 ounces of gold per year.

Over the years, they have discovered abandoned shafts as the Super Pit continues to expand. The constant digging has uncovered discarded pieces of machinery and equipment, used by the pioneer miners a century earlier. From a humble selection of wooden huts in 1903, Kalgoorlie now has a population of over 30,000 and everyone in town knows the price of gold, in the same way that mothers always know the price of a loaf of bread.

With Kalgoorlie confirmed as our destination, all I had to do was locate my rucksack and walking shorts. They were still in the garage, hanging from hooks on the wall as a reminder of my global travels with Fran. Spiders had set up home in the pack, and the boots still carried the scars of long-forgotten mountain trails.

I unhooked the shorts and traced my fingers along the patchwork of stitches holding the material together. A tailor in Zanzibar had performed major surgery on the worn fabric after they'd ripped on the upper slopes of Kilimanjaro. Feeling sentimental, I hadn't had the heart to discard them when we reached Australia.

I could still get into them, but only just! Australia had softened me a little. Maybe it was the sizeable time spent driving to work each day, or the fast-food treats and socialising most weekends. I knew the main reason. Middle age had crept up on me and I could no longer stay slim without effort. I slipped on the shorts and headed down to the beach for a run. It was late spring, and mornings were no longer cool and crisp. Within days, the temperature could creep towards the mid-thirties if the warm front continued its journey from the east.

I ran hard, my mind racing with thoughts of past adventures. As I sprinted along the water's edge, I thought back to the lioness charging in Zimbabwe, the midnight scramble towards the summit of Kilimanjaro and lazy days floating down a tributary of the Amazon. I stopped at the marina wall, fighting for breath and smiling. It was time for my next adventure.

Alan, Sam and Blake arrived from a UK winter, eager for sunshine and excitement. Blake had stretched, as all boys do when you haven't seen them in a while, but he hadn't lost his chirpy smile and mischievous giggle. Sam was still a mass of blonde curls, hugs and bright smiles. Alan hadn't changed a bit. Still the same firm handshake, cheeky grin, shaved head and thirst for adventure.

This was their first meeting with our son, Noah. At eighteen months of age, he was busy exploring his new world. With Blake on the scene, it felt like he had an older brother and they bonded instantly. Within days of touching down, Alan and Sam experienced the delights of summertime Perth, including winery tours, sunset cruises, and lazy days by the pool. Just as Alan began to get itchy feet, we prepared for our trip into the bush.

We arrived at Perth airport at the same time as hundreds of iron ore miners, all dressed in the appropriate clothes for their day ahead. Most wore fluorescent shirts, jeans and steel-capped boots as they queued for the security checks. As they neared the x-ray machines, each miner removed their boots and placed them on a conveyor, along with their phones and day-packs. There was very little talking between them, maybe because it was too early for chit-chat. Some would stay away for one or two weeks at a time, in remote mining camps, far to the north.

Our destination lay to the east, away from the ocean, towards the interior. The hour-long flight to Kalgoorlie took us over railway lines and industrial estates, towards the outer suburbs of Perth. For a while, we flew over a series of forested hills. Small communities were visible in cleared sections, but as we continued our journey, the trees dwindled from sight, replaced by pockets of farmland. Soon after, the greenery turned to an arid landscape, broken by dried riverbeds and shimmering salt lakes.

My first impression of Kalgoorlie was a good one. The sky was a perfect blue, and our taxi driver was friendly and talkative. During the brief journey from the airport to town, he had plenty of advice on where to go for entertainment, places to eat and local attractions. As a last reminder, he said, 'If you get lost, just ask for Hannan Street. It's hard to miss and has enough pubs for the two of you.'

As we pulled into our motel car park, I explained why we were in the area and asked if he knew our guide, Geoff.

'Of course,' he replied. 'There are few secrets in this town. Two degrees of separation here, mate.'

Then he said, 'I didn't know he was still a guide. Where's he taking you?'

'I'm not sure, but we'll call him later to find out.'

As we got out of the vehicle, the driver wound down his window. 'Geoff's a good bloke and is respected in the community. Stay with him and don't go wandering into the bush alone. It's gonna be hot out there during the next few days.'

He then tooted his horn and drove away as we picked up our bags and headed to the motel reception. After lazing by the pool for a few hours, we found a shopping centre nearby, offering air-conditioned comfort as we searched for somewhere to eat.

With stomachs full and time on our side, we called a taxi and drove out of town to the designated lookout point, to view the Super Pit. Before us lay a vast scar, over three kilometres long, 500 metres deep and a kilometre wide. To reduce the risk of the sides collapsing, the miners had etched wide steps into the earth. From afar, the flanks resembled the man-made terraces created by farmers in mountainous regions.

But there was no sign of plant life or greenery. They'd stripped away every piece of vegetation, revealing a Martian landscape. From our high vantage point, we could just make out the sight of yellow trucks, trundling along a winding road between the pit floor and the wide rim.

On our return to Kalgoorlie, we took a stroll in the late afternoon. Traffic was light and most cars that passed by were four-wheel drives, but unlike their shiny city equivalents, these were covered in a fine layer of red dirt. Most pedestrians seemed to be a mix of office workers, off-duty miners, and last-minute shoppers.

Just as we'd seen at Perth airport, the miners wore fluorescent shirts, steel-capped boots and long cotton trousers. They ambled at a slower pace along the wide pavements, their eyes hidden behind wraparound sunglasses. Most pedestrians avoided the glaring sun by walking close to the buildings, to take advantage of a strip of shade. We followed suit, finding ourselves outside the town hall, next to a bronze statue.

It was a replica memorial for Paddy Hannan, the most famous Irishman in Kalgoorlie, complete with his trademark brimmed hat and beard. The original sculpture was inside the town hall, made from 90 pieces of copper soldered together. The door was shut, so we stayed close to the replica, enjoying the chance to try out the additional feature of a water fountain.

On closer inspection, he looked gaunt, probably from many years in the wilderness, searching for gems. Despite the acclaim of finding and staking a claim to one of the largest gold deposits in the world, he died in 1925, leaving behind an estate valued at £1,402.

After a quick photo of Paddy's statue, we realised we were close to Hannan Street and made our way to the nearest pub. On first impressions it looked deserted, with just a handful of patrons sitting on the veranda. But as we crossed the wide road, Alan noticed a blackboard on the pavement, depicting the animated figure of a scantily clad woman. Written boldly underneath were the words, *Skimpy between 4 and 6.*

Skimpy is the term used to describe young, attractive barmaids, dressed in revealing clothes such as underwear or lingerie. Certain types of pubs employ them to entice male drinkers inside. The strategy was once common across many parts of Australia, including Perth. With the increased popularity of family-friendly pubs, scantily clad women serving from behind the counter are becoming a rare sight across most of Western Australia. Mining communities haven't dropped the practice though, and some skimpies are known to complete a circuit of the most popular drinking dens throughout the state.

We ventured inside, expecting to see a raucous group of miners ogling a scantily dressed barmaid from across the bar. Instead, we found ourselves in an open-plan room, half filled with clientele, most of whom were quietly enjoying their meals. A few men sat close to the bar, nursing glasses of beer, while in the corner, two pensioners studied the papers.

We parked ourselves on bar stools and looked around. Within a few seconds, a bright-eyed barmaid arrived to take our order. She looked to be in her early twenties and wore knee-length leather boots, a miniskirt and cropped top. Her blonde hair was pulled back in a tight bun and she had a dainty butterfly tattooed close to her navel. 'Yes, boys, what are you after?' she asked with a smile.

Alan pointed to the row of beer taps and said, 'Do you have any local ales? You know, maybe a Kalgoorlie pale ale or a craft beer?'

She gave him a cool stare, as her freckled cheeks turned rosy red. 'We sell cold beer, mate, and lots of it! We've got Swan Draught, Carlton Draught, Emu Export and more stubbies than you can shake a stick at. But we don't sell pale ales or fancy craft beers.'

Just then, a man approached the bar, dressed in a stained orange shirt, dusty jeans and work boots. Without a word, he settled himself on a nearby stool and watched as the barmaid poured him an icy beer, complete with a frothy head. He nodded in approval, peeled off a few notes and handed them over to the smiling barmaid.

She then returned her attention to Alan and said, 'Have you made your mind up yet, mate?'

He smiled easily and said, 'Well, if there isn't anything local on tap, maybe we'll try what the locals drink.'

While she poured two ice-cold beers, I felt a sudden urge to let her know about an organisation in England called CAMRA, who are fighting a just cause to educate beer drinkers on the merits of locally crafted, tasty ales. I sensed it would be a wasted conversation and waited while she placed the frothy beers on the counter. I then raised my glass to Alan in appreciation of our first beer together in the Goldfields.

Before leaving the bar, we tried chatting with the nearby miner. Alan took the initiative and asked him about his day, but with early starts and long days, it soon become clear that this was his precious time. After receiving a series of curt replies, we took the hint, headed towards the veranda and tucked into the carvery instead.

The adjacent pub had chattier clientele, with a skimpy set to show up within the hour. The resident barmaid looked attractive enough without the need to remove most of her clothes and recommended a golden ale, 'brewed in the Midwest.'

At the next pub we were offered jobs by an off-duty maintenance supervisor, because of our electrical qualifications. 'Come to Kalgoorlie and work for me,' he slurred. 'The gold price is going crazy, we're screaming for skilled people, and I hate to admit it, but you Brits are bloody good tradesmen.'

As he headed back to his mates, I realised it was time to call Geoff. Time seemed to move quickly, and the beers had flowed too easily for such an early hour. I ventured outside, drawn to the comforting sight of Paddy Hannan, and leaned against his sturdy back. For a few seconds I lingered in the warm sunshine, my head spinning lightly. I reached for my phone and called Geoff's number. As before, it seemed to take an age before he answered.

'Hello.'

'Hi, Geoff. It's Alistair, from Perth. Do you remember me?'

'Alistair. Do I know you?'

My stomach knotted, and I stood upright, walking away from Paddy while shielding my face from the sun.

'I called you a while ago, about going on a trip into the bush. I've got my friend over from England.'

His reply was gentler. 'Yes, I remember now. When are you coming to Kalgoorlie?'

'We're here now, on the eighteenth of December, just as we agreed. I'm standing in the middle of the high street, next to Paddy.'

'I thought your friend was called Alan.'

'He is. I'm standing next to the statue of Paddy Hannan.'

There was a brief pause, while Geoff digested my news. 'Do you definitely want to go? It'll be hot, you know.'

'Yes, we're here and ready. And as for the hot weather, I've been to Spain a few times during summer and coped okay, so I should be prepared for whatever comes our way!'

Geoff ignored my trip down memory lane and finished the call with a simple instruction. 'Please come and see me now. If you take a taxi to the township, we can discuss the plan.'

After collecting Alan, we detoured towards a corner shop for bottled water and then found a cab on a street corner. As we climbed into the back seats, the driver asked, 'Where to, guys?'

Alan adjusted his seat belt and chirped, 'Hello, mate, can you drop us off at the Aboriginal Township please?'

The driver craned his head towards us, his eyes narrowing. 'Are you serious?'

Alan produced a wide grin before giving an answer. 'Yes, we're going on a walkabout...'

Before Alan could explain further, the driver interrupted, his deep voice steady and clear. 'I think you've been watching too many Crocodile Dundee films, mate. The only walkabout going on around here are the locals crawling from one bloody pub to another. White men don't go to the townships. Especially those who are new to town.'

While they'd been talking, I'd drained my water bottle and contemplated going back for another one. Instead, I asked the driver if he knew an Aboriginal elder called Geoff. His voice altered a little, its gruffness easing. 'Yes, mate, he's a decent bloke and his wife is a champ.'

'Well, that's who we're visiting, and he knows we're coming.'

His brow furrowed as he mulled over the news. He then relaxed a little and reached into his top pocket as we drove out of town. 'Okay. I'll drop you off, but please take my card. If you try to walk back to Kalgoorlie afterwards, you're dafter than you look. Don't call me after eight o'clock as I won't come. I've got better things to do than track down wayward Englishmen, who want to go on a walkabout in the dark.'

The township was not far out of town and a concrete pillar marked its entrance, with the name embedded in the coarse rock. Just below, I noticed a faded sign that read, *Alcohol prohibited in the township. Always say no to drugs. Respect your family and they will respect you.*

The driver repeated his promise to return if we called before eight and dropped us off in a clearing by the gravel road. The township looked to be a circular design, with dark brick homes around the perimeter and a red brick community building in the centre. It was hard to believe we were just a 15-minute drive from one of the largest gold mines on earth, but few of the dollars from the Golden Mile seemed to have found their way into the community. Many houses were segregated by corrugated fences, with patches of wilted lawn leading to each front door. Some homes looked tired and weathered, maybe from years of extreme temperature or a lack of maintenance.

As we made our way into the centre of the township, the sound of singing grew louder. It was coming from a clearing in the gum trees and I could just make out the words to *Silent Night*, getting louder with each step we took. Many residents were lounging on chairs or rugs under the canopies of trees. On closer inspection, they turned out to be mainly women and children. The men stood on the outskirts of the grass area, their backs resting on the smooth trunks of gum trees as they listened to the music.

As far as I could see, Alan and I were the only two white faces to be seen. It was obvious we didn't belong. A pale-faced, head-shaven, six-foot Englishman and his shorter sidekick, me. In the middle of the open area stood a makeshift stage. Lined up in front were several rows of plastic chairs, some of which were already in use. Although the sun was casting long shadows of the nearby trees, the heat of the day refused to budge. I needed another drink of water and a toilet break, but neither seemed available. Instead, I tucked in behind Alan as he strode ahead, smiling at anyone who looked his way.

With each step I sensed a feeling of unease, especially from some residents, who stared ahead as we walked past. We arrived just in time to hear the last verse of *Silent Night* and found two vacant chairs in the back row. The front rows were filled, mainly by women and young children. While the adults sat and listened to the music, the toddlers crawled through gaps in the chair legs, giggling as they made their way towards the stage.

When the next song finished, the singer announced that a special guest had arrived. Somewhere in the distance, I heard the familiar roar of a motorbike and all heads turned to investigate. Father Christmas had come to town and was sitting in the sidecar of a motorbike. While the rider revved the engine and rode slowly along the gravel road, the man in costume threw sweets to the swarm of children who ran alongside, laughing and reaching out for more.

The rider stopped a few times, to allow Father Christmas the chance to throw sweets to the younger children who had been forced to the back or were still trying to catch up. After completing a circuit of the town, and with all the sweets gone, the rider tooted his horn and they were gone.

During the excitement, we heard our names being called. A dark-haired man stood behind the stage, calling us over for a chat. He wore a checked shirt and baggy trousers, but it was his bushy beard and square-rimmed glasses that held my attention. 'Welcome, my friends. I'm Geoff. I'm glad you could make it.'

He had a soft handshake, an ample girth and a hearty laugh. After exchanging pleasantries, he dropped his voice and said, 'I hope you're enjoying the evening. Thanks for coming. Please stay and listen for a while, but don't stray too far from the seats.'

Geoff's wife was one of the performers, and after a brief greeting, she returned to the stage to prepare for a duet. I sensed she was a pivotal part of the community, as was Geoff. While waiting for the children to return, Geoff began discussing the plan for our trip. 'I'll meet you tomorrow morning at nine, in the town centre by the skate park. You don't need anything except a change of clothes, a sleeping bag, a torch, and a camping knife if you have one.'

While he spoke, a group of Aboriginal men stood nearby, waiting patiently for him to finish. After our conversation, he turned to face the next in line. It seemed to me that he was a man in demand, chatting quietly with those around him. As he held counsel by the side of the stage, we returned to our seats to enjoy the carols. By the fifth song we were getting fidgety, and partway through *We Wish You a Merry Christmas,* Alan gave me a nudge. I peered around for Geoff, to say goodbye, but he was nowhere to be seen.

What we should have done at this point was head directly for the entrance, call our taxi driver and wait by the road. For some unknown reason, I convinced Alan that an evening stroll through the community to wish everybody a happy Christmas would be a spirited initiative.

We called the driver and told him we'd be at the entrance in 15 minutes, then headed towards the first set of houses. In the distance, I could see the silhouette of a group of children in the playground, blissfully unaware that their acrobatics were kicking up a cloud of red dirt. The setting sun ignited each particle, creating sparkles around their dark, gangly shapes as they leapt and cavorted in the final moments of daylight.

The first home we reached looked empty, so we continued to the second, just as the carol finished. In the silence between songs, we found ourselves outside a front garden. With no streetlights nearby, it was hard to see far, but a porch light was enough to show that there were a few people outside the front of the house.

Some were sitting quietly, while others lounged on sofas. I called out, 'Merry Christmas,' just as Geoff appeared from the trees, panting slightly. A lone voice called from the darkness, 'Nothing to see here. Please leave us alone.'

Geoff called out, 'Hey Alistair, I told you to go directly home after the carols. Come now, please.'

He quietly led us to the main road and waved us out of town a few minutes later. Our taxi driver was also quiet during the return trip to Kalgoorlie. He found his voice just as we pulled over by the statue of Paddy Hannan. 'Well, I bet that was an eye-opener for you both. Geoff is well regarded and works hard in the community. I wish I could understand the ways of the Aboriginal people a little more, but it can be a complicated topic.'

Just as we emerged from the taxi and went to pay, the driver gave us one last piece of advice. 'I'm sure you'll enjoy your time in the Goldfields and will show Geoff the respect he deserves. If I were you, I'd go easy on the beers as it will be a hot one tomorrow, especially if you're heading into the bush.'

We thanked him with a tip and went looking for something to eat. Minutes later we were in the nearest pub, standing alongside miners who'd recently finished their long shift. None had bothered to shower or change, seemingly happy to be wearing fluorescent work shirts, streaked with red dirt.

Once again, a scantily clad young barmaid came over to serve us. She didn't seem embarrassed by the little she wore, and I tried not to stare while ordering two beers. As I handed Alan his drink, an off-duty miner appeared by our side. On impulse, Alan asked him what he did for a living. The man pointed to a faded logo on his fluorescent shirt and said, 'Mate, I work for this mob, driving a truck at the gold mine and have just finished for the day.'

Alan explained that we'd been to the lookout point at the Super Pit and then asked a series of quick-fire questions. 'How big is the truck that you operate? What's it like to work at the mine? How many hours do you work each shift?'

The miner seemed happy to chat and soon let loose with some facts and figures. 'The truck is a Caterpillar 793 and it carries 225 tonnes per load. As you know, the mine is over three kilometres long and is the largest man-made hole in Australia. The job can be boring, but it pays well. I spend all day driving from the pit floor to the top and back down again.'

He'd been served a beer and took a long slurp, leaving a creamy froth on his moustache. It didn't seem to distract him, and he tugged lightly at his bushy beard as he continued. 'Mate, to tell you the truth, I play music in the cab, have air-conditioning, and somewhere in the middle of the day, stop for lunch. As long as I do my safety checks, and keep my mouth shut, I'll be set for life in ten more years.'

He looked over at the barmaid and said, 'That's if I don't blow it on beer and tips for skimpies.'

After another swig of his beer, he asked Alan, 'How much do you earn in England?'

Before Alan could answer, the miner held up a hand. 'Don't worry, bro, whatever it is, I probably earn double and only work half a year. Welcome to Australia, mate.'

He then shook our hands, picked up his beer glass and headed to the veranda, reaching for his cigarettes as he went. We went in the opposite direction, towards the meal counter and just made last orders before the chef headed home. With a long day ahead, we finished our meals and strolled outside in search of one more location on our wish-list, a pink and white building known as Questa Casa.

In the darkness, the corrugated iron cladding gave the establishment the look of an antiquated motel block, although it is renowned as being the oldest working brothel in Australia and also a popular tourist attraction. We weren't after much, just an impromptu tour and a cup of tea. After ringing the bell, the door opened, to reveal a red-haired woman in a floral dressing gown. We soon discovered that late night tours and refreshments were off the menu. With a weary smile, she closed the door, leaving us on the street.

We woke to another clear sky and finished the in-house orange juice while listening to the news. Perth Airport was experiencing flight delays and the weather reporter was predicting a high of 38 degrees by midday. After breakfast, we made our way into the town, which was eerily quiet after the hustle and bustle of the previous evening.

As before, most cars that passed by were lightly coated in red dirt. I made a mental note to see if Kalgoorlie had an automatic car-washing facility, as there was definitely a business case for one. Alan woke me from my daydream when he asked, 'Ali, how much do you know about Geoff?'

I looked up at his face and grinned. 'As much as you do.'

'Do you think he'll turn up?'

I smiled again and said, 'Absolutely.'

For a moment, he had a rare, serious look. 'I reckon we need to buy all our own water. Just in case.'

We emerged from the nearest corner shop, laden down with large bottles of mineral water, and walked towards the agreed meeting place. The sun was climbing steadily, its powerful rays forcing us to don hats to protect our shaved heads. Traffic was light and most vehicles that passed by looked capable of heading off-road. Some had flashing beacons and fluorescent stripes, to prepare for their time in the Super Pit or other nearby mine sites.

The next off-road vehicle didn't continue, but veered left and came to a stop. At the wheel was Geoff, his wide grin impossible to miss. He wound the window down, suppressing the need to laugh. 'Why have you brought your own water? We have plenty.'

Riding shotgun was another man, far younger, and probably in his early twenties. They both got out of the car and Geoff introduced him as Ben, his son. Aboriginals do not attempt bone-crunching handshakes. It's not their custom. Ben was softly spoken, as was his handshake. His soft curls were trimmed short and most were hidden behind a bright red baseball cap. He helped load our luggage onto the roof rack and then silently returned to the front seat. Geoff remained outside on the pavement and asked, 'Are you two going somewhere afterwards?'

Alan stared at the bags and said, 'No, Geoff, just back to Perth.'

'Then why did you pack for a month and bring so much water?'

He patted Alan on the back and chuckled. 'I'm only joking, my friends. Hop in. It's time to go.'

We soon drove past the pubs and restaurants, but they were closed for now and the mobile billboards advertising skimpies had been stashed away. Within minutes, we were on the outskirts of town and still hadn't passed any pedestrians. Geoff drove for a few more kilometres, then took a turning onto a gravel track, which prompted Alan to call out from the rear seats. 'What's the plan for today, Geoff?'

He pointed towards a line of trees and said, 'We'll head into the bush, to some out-of-the-way places. Then we can go in search of something to eat.'

Alan peered outside and said, 'That sounds great, although I have no idea which way we're heading, as it all looks the same to me.'

Geoff couldn't hold back a smile as he replied, 'That's the problem with you people from the city. You're not looking properly. Look, here's our track now.'

I didn't see a track, just scrubland and bushes. Geoff left the gravel road and drove straight towards them, laughing as we bounced around in the back seats. On the other side of the rise was more scrubland, but he seemed to have a sixth sense for where to drive and ploughed forward. It was too noisy for meaningful conversation, so for the first hour we sat quietly in the back as the Toyota travelled along a labyrinth of trails.

During this time, I tried calculating our direction of travel by studying the sun, but the rising heat inside the car soon distracted me. The air was filling with airborne particles of dirt, sucked in through a tiny gap from a side window. Although the cooling fan was cranked to the maximum, it did little to ease the rising temperature. By now, I realised that I'd stored my personal water bottle with my belongings on the roof rack.

The water bottles that Alan had wanted were strewn across the floor, so I leaned down to grab one. Geoff caught the movement in his rear-view mirror and said, 'Good idea, Alistair. When you're ready, pass one up front.'

I took a gulp of mine and handed another towards him. Initially, he sat the container between his legs and then took long sips whenever the road levelled out. By the time we'd traversed a sandy ridge, the bottle was drained. He handed it back and called out with a cheer. 'I'm glad you both brought plenty of spring water with you.'

Ben remained quiet, listening to music through his earphones as we drove into the unknown. The sun was high by now and my stomach was demanding food. I had a stash of ginger-nut biscuits in my rucksack for emergency situations, plus a banana in my day bag, which I sensed was already squashed. Alan sat alongside me, watching the world pass by as we continued along the rutted path. With impeccable timing, Geoff slowed the car and called out, 'I think it's time to find something to eat.'

The vehicle came to a stop and we clambered out. We were in a pocket of woodland, with no obvious sign of a track, and it seemed to me that Geoff was forging his own path into the wilderness. He opened the boot, pulled out a shovel and a knife, and then handed them to Alan. 'Okay, now we'll dig for witchetty grubs. I hope you're both hungry.'

Witchetty grubs live in the root of the witchetty tree and for thousands of years have been an important part of the Aboriginal diet during their trips into the hinterland. They are a ready-made meal, bursting with protein, and can be enjoyed by anyone who knows where to forage. After a few simple instructions from Geoff, we got to our knees and scraped away the dried grass and mud.

Alan seemed determined to dig deeper and within minutes had found the roots. Geoff helped him pull the nearest root and pointed towards a slight bump. 'Good job, Alan. This is where the grub lives.'

He asked Alan to slice the root and as he did so, the grub eased out. As it plopped into Alan's hand, I studied the docile creature, which resembled a plump hairless caterpillar, without legs. It was greyish brown, squishy to touch and as wide as Alan's thumb.

Geoff picked it from Alan's hand, popped it into his mouth, chewed for a few moments and said, 'Delicious. Now it's your turn.'

We all took turns digging for roots and found enough grubs to fill a plate. While we'd been coaxing them from the roots, Ben had started a contained fire, and after rinsing the end of the shovel with water, placed it in the flames. Once it was hot, he seared the grubs and offered them up for eating. They slid down easily, crunchy on the outside, soft in the middle, with an aftertaste of muddy walnuts.

I tried eating another grub, this time between two gingernut biscuits, hoping to create an improvised custard cream. I decided afterwards that witchetty grubs were best for emergencies and washed away the bitter aftertaste with a mouthful of spring water. A rumbling stomach led me to my bruised banana, and as I chomped happily, Geoff appeared on the scene. 'Hey, Alistair, I've got something tastier than that. Come on–let's open the provisions.'

After filling up on bread, crackers, cheese and ham, we continued our journey. Although Geoff seemed relaxed at the wheel, I was never sure if he was following ancient game trails passed down from his ancestors, or just trailblazing through dense bush, hoping to find a place to hunt and camp. My doubts were eased when we came to a wide escarpment at the edge of a dried riverbed and stopped the vehicle. He smiled and said, 'Come, my friends, I will show you a special place.'

As we walked along the rocky outcrop, he spoke bluntly to us. 'You won't understand most of what I say because many white men are not connected with the land. But I will try to explain. This is my ancestral land. I know every rock, tree, and game trail. My family has hunted here for generations, and contrary to what you read and hear, many indigenous Australians are still connected with the land.'

Until recently, the Aboriginal people had an affinity with the land that most westerners have long forgotten or never had. I am no expert on the effects of colonisation on indigenous populations, but since moving to Australia, this was the first person I'd met who spoke passionately about the environment in which he lived.

He spoke briefly about the Dreamtime, a term used for describing when the land and people were created by the Spirits at the beginning of time. But as I probed further, his voice rose and fell as we clambered over rocks towards an ancient watercourse. Just ahead sat a dried-up lake, shimmering in the midday sun.

Geoff encouraged us to sit in silence while taking in the view. Initially, the land before me looked barren, but as each minute passed, I caught sight of insects and birds and heard the scurry of a lizard across nearby rocks. While studying a bird in flight, I caught sight of a larger creature, this time on land. An animal was heading towards the tree line, and by the way it moved, was four-legged.

'It's a dingo,' Geoff explained. 'Or maybe just a wild dog. It's hard to know from this far away. Come on, it is time to go. We have a lot more places to visit before the day is through.'

As Geoff stood to leave, I studied the faraway creature. It seemed to sense my eyes were upon it and stopped at the edge of the trees to gaze back. For a few seconds we stared at each other from afar, with the dried lake between us. Maybe we were not so different after all. It was either a wild dog, a dingo or a mix of both, searching for food and shelter. I was English born, to an Irish mother and Scottish father, looking to settle in a new country.

While walking back to the vehicle, I thought back to Geoff's comments about some white men not having a true affinity with the land. It was a sweeping statement, but hadn't been said in malice. I knew it wasn't true and had met numerous people in Ecuador who were determined to restore the ravaged jungles, and many of those passionate individuals were from western countries. To Geoff, it was just a simple fact that too many people are out of sync with the natural world.

By mid-afternoon we were trailblazing through rockier country, and after many sightings of wallabies, Geoff slowed down in search of dinner. Just as we rounded a bend, he came to a stop and called out for attention. 'Hey, there's a goanna. Can you see it?'

He pointed through the windscreen, but all I could see were trees, shrubs, red dirt and boulders. 'There it is. Just there,' he whispered.

The more he pointed, the less I saw, and Alan also shook his head in puzzlement. Geoff got out of the car, quietly made his way towards the bonnet and once more pointed towards the boulders. I leaned close to the window, my eyes peeled for signs of the goanna, but there didn't seem to be anything there. Geoff came back to his seat, shaking his head in disappointment. 'You need to look with bush eyes, not city eyes. Please watch where I am pointing.'

As Geoff returned to the front of the vehicle, I wound the side window down and craned my head to get a better view of the rocky outcrop. With bright sunshine and the drone of insects it was hard to concentrate, but Geoff was waiting for the thumbs up, and I didn't want to let him down. As I watched, he picked up a rock and dropped his voice to a whisper. 'Watch where it lands, as it will scare it off.'

He threw the rock towards the boulders, where it landed with a thud and clattered away. In the silence that followed, nothing moved, except Geoff, mumbling to himself as he stepped towards the boulders and picked up a stunned goanna by the tail. The lizard flopped by his side, its head dangling close to the ground. 'I'm not a good shot,' he bellowed. 'I've knocked it out, but I think we'll have it for dinner.'

In one swift motion, he gripped the tail and spun the creature in a perfect arc, so that its head landed squarely on the bonnet of the car. The impact killed the reptile immediately, its skull split in two. He opened the back door, placed the goanna next to Alan's feet and said, 'Here's our starters for dinner.'

The area turned out to be a perfect habitat for goannas. Soon after, we spotted another one, lazing on a granite outcrop, soaking up the mid-afternoon sunshine. It was larger than the first, about a metre long, and lifted its head to investigate the vibrating noise from the diesel engine. Geoff had his rifle ready and took a shot from his window with deadly accuracy. Within seconds, we had a second goanna lying by our feet.

An hour before sunset, we approached a wide-open patch of ground, which Geoff confirmed would be our campsite. Once again, Ben soon had a fire going, and as the shadows from nearby trees lengthened, Alan and I explored the area. Kangaroos kept their distance, bouncing away from view as soon as we approached. The land nearby was littered with remnants of human habitation, left behind by prospectors and campers.

Each contour and ridge contained something from the past–a dented tin mug, now home to a patrolling army ant, smashed cups, broken beer bottles, rusted cans and fragments of discarded clothes. I felt a tinge of sadness at the human waste left behind, some dating back many years. We didn't have the space on board to take it away, or the time to scoop it all up. Instead, I picked up an empty beer bottle as a token gesture and placed it in my rucksack.

Further exploration revealed many boreholes and the visible remains of an abandoned tenement. Compared to the suburban streets of Perth, the open sky seemed vast, with no buildings or artificial light to taint the view. For a few minutes we kicked at the dirt, hoping for signs of gold, but Geoff called our names from afar and our brief exploration was over. It was time for dinner.

As the sun dropped towards the horizon, the flies vanished. For the first time in hours, I could talk without waving my hands in front of my face. In the last of the light, Geoff sat by the fireside and explained how to prepare the goannas for cooking. Far above, a thin trail of clouds turned from white to pink to velvet red, as the sky flared briefly before darkness descended.

In the soft glow of the firelight, Geoff took out his knife and made an inch wide incision below the throat of the smallest lizard and then snapped a barbed twig from a nearby bush. While we watched, he eased the twig into the opening and pushed it towards the belly. 'All you do now is gently twist a few times, before pulling it out.'

He handed the goanna to Alan, who pulled out the snagged entrails in one go. Geoff patted him on the back and said, 'You seem like a natural. Just one more to go between the two of you. When they're gutted, lay them near the edge of the fire to cook.'

He then made his way to the vehicle to prepare beans and pasta, leaving me and Alan to prepare the meat. He returned soon after and gave a nod of approval, apart from the blood-stained innards by the fireside. These, we discovered, could attract ants, snakes, wild dogs or dingoes.

Instead of throwing them into the fire, I scooped them with a stick and headed into the darkness. My head torch picked out two kangaroos in the distance, their ears perked in anticipation as I approached. They took flight, crashing through the bush. As the world turned silent, I dropped the entrails, then switched off my light.

The faint glow from the fire failed to reach me, and just like my time in Africa, I felt like an explorer. This time I was not in the wilds of Botswana or Tanzania, but a short flight and a day's drive from the largest city in Western Australia.

We ate in silence around the campfire. I was too tired for small talk and too hungry to complain about the over-cooked pasta. The goanna was delicious, as most food is to a ravenous person. I figured it tasted like chicken used to, before they introduced hormones, and its earthy flavour complemented the baked beans and sticky pasta.

With no moon or artificial light, the night was as black as I'd hoped. At the edge of camp, Alan and I lay on our mats and gazed up at the Milky Way, eager to point out satellites and the Southern Cross. As we searched for shooting stars, Geoff appeared from the bush, his heavy footsteps intruding on the still of night. He was holding one of our bottles of water, its final contents swirling in the bottom.

'Thanks for today,' Alan called out.

'No worries, my friends, sleep well. I have swept the camp clear of ants and etched a mark around the perimeter. Don't worry—nothing will cross the line during the night.'

I didn't quite know what he was expecting to come into camp, but guessed he meant unwelcome wildlife. I was unsure how a slight indent in the earth would stop an army of ants or an inquisitive snake. I should have asked but felt too tired to dwell on the fact that the Australian outback is home to some of the deadliest wildlife on the planet! Alan seemed unconcerned about any apparent danger and was now happily reading a book by torchlight. I lay on the ground nearby, swaddled deep inside my sleeping bag, and searched for one more shooting star in the night sky.

While drifting to sleep, my mind wandered back to my travels in South America. I dreamt of Carlos, my Peruvian guide, and his trusty donkeys who I'd nicknamed Angus and Oliver. Where were they all now? During my reverie, Carlos appeared from the wilderness, his donkeys tethered after a day's trekking across the Andes. He whispered something to me in Spanish, but I didn't understand, so he took my hand and led me to a wide river, surrounded by snow-capped peaks.

As I sat by the water's edge, he cast his fishing rod into clear pools at the edge of the river and began reeling in trout. Soon, he'd caught enough for a meal and carried them over for me. As he approached, the dream began fading and I could no longer hear his words.

Sometime later, I heard another noise. Instead of Carlos, I heard a shrill buzzing, which woke me with a start. As I opened my eyes, all became clear. The sun was low on the horizon, Geoff was standing close by, and the first fly of the day was investigating one of my ears.

We enjoyed a relaxed morning at camp, with a breakfast of fried eggs and bacon, washed down with coffee. Afterwards, Alan and I took a walk into the surrounding bushland to explore the abandoned tenements. The rising sun and persistent flies chased away any notion of staying too long. As soon as Geoff beeped the horn of his vehicle, we were nearby and ready.

Once inside, we asked for the air conditioning to be cranked to its maximum. While Ben reached for the dial, Alan leaned forward and asked, 'Where to today then, Geoff?'

'We're heading into the bush again, which will take us to a remote town that I think you'll both enjoy.'

And with that, he set off from camp. All morning, we drove along rutted tracks in search of our next dinner. Geoff kept mumbling something about kangaroos, but the wooded terrain gave few clues to their whereabouts. Occasionally, he'd slow down and call for a water bottle, as the temperature continued to rise. I must have dozed off until Alan woke me with a tap on the shoulder. 'Hey, Ali, wake up. Look. It's a road.'

I opened my eyes and spotted a fence, a gate and a scrawny goat. I wiped sweat from my brow, then looked again and they were gone. Up ahead lay a narrow road, its black tarmac weathered and worn, with deep cracks and potholes. As we weaved around each hole, I leaned towards the front seats and said, 'This looks interesting. Where are we, Geoff?'

'We're approaching an old mining town called Kookynie. I bet you boys want a cold beer, eh?'

Alan cracked a mischievous smile and said, 'Sounds like a plan, Geoff. I thought you'd never ask!'

I wasn't sure if Geoff was jesting, as the chances of finding a pub seemed remote in such an area. But as the road widened and the cracks vanished, the sight of a lonely roundabout gave a glimmer of hope. The first signpost in two days revealed our distance to the nearest communities, most of which were tiny settlements in the vast interior.

As Geoff slowed, I opened my guidebook and searched for information about the town. A quick read revealed that the population of Kookynie was just 13, but there was no sight of anyone as we entered the main street. Maybe the residents were all in the pub or out in the wilderness, searching for gold. We passed a row of abandoned brick houses, their sealed windows hiding any secrets of the original inhabitants. My book referred to Kookynie as a mining town, but as we drove down the desolate strip, there was little sign of activity.

Up ahead, there was one building that stood like a shining beacon. The Grand Hotel Kookynie resembled an oasis in the desert, complete with a hanging basket of colourful daisies cascading towards the entrance doorway. After Geoff parked the vehicle, we all got out to stretch our legs. I stepped into the road and looked around for signs of traffic but nothing stirred in the heat, except the persistent flies.

Geoff pointed to the hotel and said, 'You boys need to get inside, out of the heat. Take your time and enjoy a drink. I'll be out here, with Ben.'

'Do you fancy a drink as well?' Alan asked. 'Even just a cold lemonade or something?'

Ben held up his hand and smiled. 'No, we're good, thanks. Like my dad said, you take your time and we'll be here, waiting.'

There was a moment when nobody moved or spoke. They had their reasons for not going into the hotel bar and it wasn't for me or Alan to pry further. We'd have preferred their company but didn't ask again.

Instead, we made our way across the dusty road towards the hotel. Someone had propped a side door open with a boot-sized lump of iron ore, and as we approached, I heard music coming from the other side of a screen door. After stepping into the cool interior, the sound of Glen Campbell welcomed us, singing a country classic. In such a remote and arid location, I'd been expecting to find an establishment on its last legs. Instead, we stepped into a furnished hallway and made our way towards the front bar.

The place was empty, which didn't surprise me, as there were no other vehicles outside except ours. What it lacked in people, it made up with décor and ambience. A selection of spirits, cigarettes, potato chips and peanuts were displayed across the back of the bar. For those in need of other items, there was a limited choice of tinned food, magazines and newspapers. On one shelf sat a packet of two-minute noodles. The walls were decorated with retro images of Australian football posters, beer mats, and faded postcards from across the world.

We each sat on a bar stool, just as a barman appeared from the back room and greeted us with a friendly, 'G'day.' He was about 50, quiet voiced with a stringy grey beard, and asked us what we were after. Alan smiled at the barman before turning his attention to the beers on offer. 'Hello, mate, do you have any locally brewed beer?'

The barman put his hand on the nearest beer tap, which was coated in a layer of ice, and looked Alan in the eye. 'We've got plenty of beer, mate. All ice cold. If you want something different, I can sell you an expensive bottle of beer that the Mexicans drink after they've been surfing. Other than that, you can take your pick.'

The choice of beers on tap was limited, but in a ghost town you can't be too picky. My guess is that after twelve hours sifting through dirt in blood boiling temperatures to find a speck of gold, you don't care so much about the taste. It just has to be cold enough to lubricate a parched throat. We each chose a tall glass of Swan Draught, and as he poured I enquired about the two-minute noodles, as our evening meal was by no means guaranteed!

While Alan chatted with the barman about the merits of English craft beer, I took a stroll to the toilet, passing framed photos of days long past when Kookynie was a pioneer town in the grip of a gold frenzy. It would have been an amazing time to be in mid-west Australia, akin to the Californian gold rush of the mid-nineteenth century. The pictures were in excellent condition, as was the décor, and it was clear that the owner was proud of the hotel's heritage.

By the time I returned, another drink had been served, and the barman looked to be enjoying the banter. As I've mentioned before, Alan is an asset to any trip, as he can cajole most people into an easy conversation. As they talked about the price of gold and the last significant discovery, I studied the solitary packet of noodles. They were a little out of date, but by nightfall, if it was those or witchetty grub custard creams, I knew which one would win my vote.

After I'd purchased the noodles, the barman continued with the lively chat. 'I've read in some guidebooks that there are 13 people in town but it's less than that now. There has been the occasional argument over the years between the regulars, probably over mining rights or a card game, but they mostly stick to themselves. Some live nearby, while others just come and go with the seasons.'

Alan grinned and took a sip of beer as the barman continued. 'When they come in, they mostly sit where you are now. They don't bother so much during the weekends as it's filled with blow-ins, like you two. I sometimes get unexpected visitors such as retirees on caravanning trips, or overseas travellers that have hired a car for the day from Kalgoorlie.'

These types of visitors were his financial lifeline, but the wandering Australians were the ones I wanted to meet. They were an elusive bunch, and as we finished our drinks, I thought about my next adventure, in search of these larrikins.

As we finished our drinks, the barman gave us a quick history lesson and revealed that he was also the hotel owner. With a sense of pride, he reeled off a series of facts and figures about the glory days of gold mining in the area. During the boom years at the turn of the twentieth century, the town had 3,500 residents, 11 hotels and an active train line to Kalgoorlie. It also had a racecourse, delicatessens, factories, a red-light district and the first swimming baths in Western Australia.

The major reason that such a large population lived in the town was the riches on offer. In Kookynie, fortunes were found, but many came away as losers. Over the years, the mine suffered from serious flooding, along with fluctuating gold prices and richer pickings elsewhere. The mine limped along for several years, but the population drifted away. By the 1960s, the school had closed, and most residents had left. Lone prospectors still roam the area, spending weeks, months and years in the wilderness, searching for gold or precious stones.

As he spoke, I wondered if Paddy Hannan had ever drunk at the same bar where we were now sitting. I could imagine the animated conversations each evening, as travellers, prospectors and drifters discussed the latest gold findings, each tale a little taller than the last.

After thanking the owner, we stood to leave. He handed me the noodles and explained that he had to head to the kitchen, to prepare dinner for some overseas visitors who were driving from Kalgoorlie. It felt good knowing the hotel would soon be alive with the sound of chatter and laughter. After reaching the doorway, I stopped to take a last look around the bar, feeling grateful for the chance to have enjoyed a few yarns in such historical surrounds. We then waved farewell and stepped out of the cool interior, into blazing sunshine.

Before coming to Kalgoorlie, it had been many years since I'd walked out of a pub with Alan during the middle of the day.

A summer holiday in Tenerife would have been our previous attempt at a lunchtime session, and that had been a long time ago. We were still clinging to hair at the time and had taken a break from the car factory to enjoy a week of sunshine and partying on the island with friends. But the factory was now shut, and our hair was no more. Yet here we were, still seeking adventures, this time on the other side of the world.

That afternoon, we set up camp by a dam. By sunset, we were fishing for freshwater crustaceans, known as yabbies. We used a net and trap, which Geoff had stashed on his roof rack in preparation. Using tiny strips of goanna as bait, Geoff entrusted us with pulling the lines in at regular intervals. The water must have been teeming with the creatures, who were still nibbling at the stringy meat as we emptied each catch into a bucket. On closer inspection, they looked to be a cross between prawns and crabs. That evening, as we feasted on boiled yabbies, the two-minute noodles became a distant memory.

Once again, we crawled into our sleeping bags for a deep sleep under the stars, and this time my dreams were serene. On the morning of the third day, I spotted Geoff by the campfire, staring across the broken ground.

'Is everything okay?' I asked.

My words seemed to shake him out of a daydream, and he turned to face me, his frizzy hair now wild and unkempt. He pointed towards the horizon and gave a hearty chuckle. 'Today, we're gonna get ourselves a roo.'

He prepared his rifle, and after a breakfast of scrambled eggs, we headed into the bush in high anticipation. All morning we drove along game trails, but the kangaroos proved to be elusive, either resting undetected or grazing in pockets of woodland. Basking reptiles were ignored in favour of distant kangaroos, but each foray across the bush ended in dismay.

We ate cheese, crackers and dried fruit for morning tea, and then went in search of another witchetty tree. Along the way, Geoff spotted a bush turkey foraging in the scrub. With the accuracy of a marksman, he dropped it from afar with his high-velocity rifle. After being plucked, gutted and grilled, it soon complemented the two-minute noodles, bread and baked beans.

After we'd packed up and returned to the vehicle, Geoff called out for us to keep our eyes peeled for larger game. The sun was at its peak now, and despite the high-pitched whining from the air conditioner, the temperature continued to climb. It was the first time since leaving Kalgoorlie that I realised we were all in need of a shower. Despite the whiff of sweat in the close confines, we remained a happy-go-lucky bunch, as Geoff navigated the trails in search of a kangaroo.

Alan sat alongside me, wearing the same mud-stained T-shirt as the previous day. His unshaven face was smeared with red dirt, but he didn't seem to mind. Instead, he smiled back at me, seeing that I was in similar shape, and returned to his book as we rolled with the bumps.

Ben remained quiet, taking the job of riding shotgun seriously as we studied the wooded terrain for signs of life. Just as Geoff called for another water bottle, he changed his mind and eased the vehicle to a stop. 'Look over there. What can you see under the tree?'

I looked all around for signs of life, but in the shimmering haze, very little stirred. My eyes focused on the gum tree that Geoff had pointed out, but all I could see was a torn branch, resting in the scrub. I ignored the sweat running down my back and waved away a fly to concentrate further. Suddenly, I spotted a slight movement. Was it the flicker of an ear? All small talk vanished–the only sound now was the thudding drumbeat of the engine.

I thought back to Geoff's words from a few days earlier. About looking with city eyes. I blinked the sweat away and concentrated on the splintered branch. It was no longer a piece of rotting timber. At last, I could see the outline of a kangaroo's head. It moved again, revealing two ears and a prominent nose. It then stood tall to investigate the unnatural noise. Geoff had found his kangaroo.

Even from afar, I could sense that it was about to flee. But a twitch of the ears was the last movement it ever made. Geoff had already steadied his rifle, and as the animal stared ahead, the crack of gunfire broke the silence. Far in the distance at that moment, the kangaroo's head whipped back as it keeled over.

With ringing in my ears, we sped to the kill site, as Geoff didn't want it to suffer. There was no need for haste, as the headshot had been clean. It was a fully grown grey kangaroo, now flat on its back. He stowed the rifle, sliced off the tail and stored it in the rear of the vehicle. Before I could ask questions, he called out, 'It's time to find a big tree.'

Geoff and Ben trussed a rope around the carcass, then asked for help in getting it onto the bonnet. Alan pulled a leg, and I pushed from the rear until we had it laid flat across the vehicle, with its head resting on the windscreen. Flies were already buzzing around the kangaroo, despite it being dead for less than a few minutes. As soon as we drove off, they vanished.

With every bump, the kangaroo rolled back and forth and looked in danger of falling off the bonnet. As Geoff found his tree and came to a stop, the flies returned and swarmed around the carcass. Geoff slung a rope over the thickest branch and asked for help with hauling the kangaroo high. Now I understood why he needed a decent-sized tree!

While Ben searched for a clearing to start a campfire, Geoff gutted the kangaroo, ignoring the cloud of flies that hovered around him. He was in the zone now, his honed knife slicing through the coarse skin to find the succulent meat. While he worked, we set up the table and chairs in anticipation.

After I'd cleaned the table, Geoff appeared by my side, grinning. A glistening lump of raw meat was skewered on his blade, which he flicked onto the damp surface, followed soon after by many more. Before the flies could make their move, Geoff prompted us into action. 'Okay, lads, it's time to grab your meat and roast it on the fire.'

After we'd eaten, Geoff took a drive towards distant rocks and asked me to join him. Along the way he said, 'Out here in the bush, it's important to give and take. There are goannas nearby and they'll appreciate the meal.'

He then parked by the boulders and placed two large chunks of raw meat onto the ground. That evening, we camped well away from the carcass and enjoyed a hearty stew of diced kangaroo, potatoes and carrots, simmered in a pot over the fire. As a last touch, we added local herbs to enhance the flavour. While we ate, Geoff touched on the subject of the Dreamtime again.

Eager to learn, I asked questions and probed for answers. But the replies were too vague, and I sensed we were being slightly teased. Geoff picked up on this and changed his tone. Eventually he just said, 'You two are good, because you listen. I reckon if you stay with me for a few months, you'd understand. But city people are always in a hurry and rarely learn about our ways.'

And with that, he got up to stretch and then strolled towards the nearest trees. Just before we turned in for the night, he collected the kangaroo tail, wrapped it in foil and buried it in the embers at the edge of the fire. He noticed me watching and smiled. 'This is my breakfast, Ali. Out here in the bush, you have to think ahead.'

Later, as I lay on my sleeping mat, watching for shooting stars, I looked over at Alan. He was nibbling a cold turkey fillet, chuckling out loud while reading his book by torchlight.

Sunrise dictates life in the bush, so bright sunshine and buzzing flies meant another early start to the day. After breakfast, we dampened down the fire and set off once more. Two kilometres down the track Geoff stopped the vehicle and turned in his seat. 'Hey, Alan. Did you take the kangaroo tail out of the embers this morning?'

In reply, Alan shook his head and said, 'No, Geoff. Was I meant to?'

A sharp U-turn meant the answer was yes. After collecting the roasted tail, Geoff relaxed at the wheel, as we made our way back to civilisation. Fenced paddocks appeared, housed with skinny goats and gaunt cattle, but the area still seemed devoid of people. The sight of power lines meant the trip was all but over. They were running parallel with a wide bitumen road and I knew it wouldn't be long before we arrived in Kalgoorlie.

We stopped once more, so Geoff could enjoy his roasted kangaroo tail. As we sat by the roadside, he offered me a portion while reminding me that some people consider it to be a delicacy. Instead, I declined the offer and thought ahead to a pub meal at the Exchange Hotel. By mid-afternoon, we drove through the streets of Kalgoorlie once more. Although I'd only been away for a short while, I somehow felt more connected with the city, as though I'd earned my stripes to be there.

Before dropping us off, Geoff detoured towards his home to meet the rest of his family. Afterwards, he drove us to the community hall where he proudly showed us some projects he was working on. When it came time to say goodbye, I didn't know whether to softly shake his hand or grip him in a bear hug.

Without doubt, the trip had been one of the most memorable of my life. Not only had I rekindled my friendship with Alan, but I'd also learned a few snippets about life in the outback and the ways of the Aboriginal people. For sure, I was just a beginner with lots to learn, but it felt good to know that I'd started the journey.

Just before we left the hall, Alan spotted a visitor's book. With promises to return it soon, he tucked it under his arm as we strolled towards the nearest pub. We couldn't have timed it better. Happy hour had just started and as we walked into the front bar, we recognised the skimpy from our previous visit. She wore a similar outfit, just as revealing, but had replaced her leather boots with sandals.

Three days without a shower had left its mark on us, but we wore our red sheen with pride and plonked down on the nearest bar stools. The place was quiet, except for a few pensioners playing cards and an off-duty miner sitting alone in the corner. The barmaid came over to where we sat and asked, 'Yes, boys, what are you after?'

Alan ran his fingers over the thin coat of ice on the nearest beer tap and said, 'Two of your coldest beers, please.'

She studied us again, then smiled warmly. 'You're both learning fast and it looks like you've been busy since we last met.'

Alan grinned and muttered something about prospecting for gold. She'd heard it all before and didn't raise an eyebrow while expertly pouring two icy beers. Later, while the chef prepared steak, mushrooms and chips, we took our drinks out on the veranda, along with the visitor's book. By the time the meal was finished, we'd written a poem:

Out in Kalgoorlie, we met two Aboriginal men
    One called Geoff, the other one, Ben
    Geoff tempted us away from the Hannan street pubs
    To sample kangaroo meat and witchetty grubs
    He promised us bush tucker and was true to his word
    So, in the pot that night sat a bush turkey bird
    Yes, Geoff is a legend, and he showed us his home
    Taking us to the places where his family once roamed
    So, thanks for the experience and the education at that
    We're off home to explore the garden and hunt for the neighbour's cat

On our return to Perth, the festive season was in full swing, with blue skies and high temperatures forecast for the week ahead. Inflatable Santas were a common sight across suburban gardens, and I also spotted fluorescent snowmen and flashing reindeer during a night time drive with the children.

Partway through Christmas morning, Noah and Blake were prised away from their presents, in exchange for a smothering of sunscreen and the chance to each wear a Santa hat while on Mullaloo beach, 20 minutes north of the city centre. After loading up with towels, ball games and refreshments, both families left behind the cool comfort of an air-conditioned lounge for a drive to the coast, hoping to beat the heat, traffic and crowds.

We arrived at nine and squeezed into the last remaining parking spots, before venturing across parkland towards a life-saving club overlooking the Indian Ocean. Two weeks earlier, the same stretch of beach had been empty, apart from a handful of children enjoying the waves. Now, on Christmas Day, the scene had changed, with hundreds of people lounging on towels and many more in transit along a coastal path, all looking to stake their claim.

As we stepped barefoot onto the sand, I spotted a young couple, lean and tanned, strolling hand in hand–dressed in matching baseball caps, bathers and long-sleeved shirts–each holding a towel, a paperback and water bottle. Languishing behind, was a middle-aged couple in shorts and T-shirts, dragging a four wheeled buggy through the sand. It was filled with balls, fishing rods, camping chairs, towels and a bright yellow duck, fully inflated and ready to be launched.

On closer inspection, the buggy had other goodies, including a sea blue awning, still crammed in its cardboard box. Pride of place went to the two young children, dressed in swimwear and elf hats, while sitting on top of an insulated container the size of a bar fridge. Their oldest sibling was scouting the sandy foreground, his eyes darting between the ocean and a group of teenage girls lying like sardines in a can across a mosaic of towels.

While Fran searched for a vacant spot away from the family of five, I overheard accents from across England, Scotland, Ireland, and Wales. Some beach goers had planted colourful flags, depicting the town or city where they came from back home, or the football club they supported. Now I knew where many of the ex-pats visited each Christmas Day!

With no flags to plant, our setup was easy and after we'd laid a blanket across the flattened sand, Noah and Blake made a smart move towards the ocean, followed closely by their mothers! Alan led the way, adjusting his swimming goggles while wading into deeper water. With promises to join them soon, I strolled along the shoreline in my new bathing shorts, Hawaiian shirt, Santa hat and shades! Along the way, I heard pop music pulsating from portable speakers, competing with Christmas carols and the sound of laughter.

With so many British and Irish flags within view, along with familiar accents, instead of Perth, Western Australia, I could have been in Majorca on a summer holiday. There were Celtic fans lying close to a family of four from Liverpool and two pale girls sprawled on towels alongside an Irish flag. Further on, I spotted a group of youths playing beach volleyball alongside an Arsenal flag, surprisingly close to a barrel-chested man wearing a Spurs football top.

After a dip in the ocean and the chance to play with Noah and Blake, I watched as friends posed for selfies by the water's edge, with promises to send each photo to the folks back home, shivering through another long winter. There was talk about grey skies above London, powerful winds pounding the shores of Galway and the promise of snow for those in the Highlands of Scotland. In comparison, the residents of Perth had been warned by the met office about the perils of sunbathing for too long on Christmas Day, with the thermometer set to nudge the high thirties by mid-afternoon.

Within two hours of our arrival, we called it a day, waved goodbye to newfound friends and made our escape from the sunshine. While strolling across the beach, I spotted the family of five, huddled together while sheltering under their new awning. Each wore a Santa hat as they tucked into drinks and nibbles while listening to Christmas tunes, surrounded by mountains of wrapping paper, discarded fishing rods and a bright yellow duck, lying lifeless and punctured across the sand.

Just before sunset, Alan fired up the barbeque, for a banquet of grilled chicken, tiger prawns and crayfish, washed down with ice-cold drinks. After putting the children to bed, the conversation turned to our week-long holiday to the southwest of Australia, planned to begin on Boxing Day!

The region is renowned for its world-class wineries, towering forests, pristine beaches and epic surf breaks. In the summer months it attracts visitors from across the world, who mingle alongside the locals while soaking up the sunshine. Some go for the surf, others for the mountain bike trails, coastal footpaths or fishing spots. The country town of Margaret River is renowned as being the central hub for many of the attractions and activities. It is also famed for holding the Margaret River Pro, an annual event in the World Surfing Tour calendar which shines a light on this special part of Australia.

For those in search of a slower pace, the choices on offer include coffee shops, wineries, family-friendly breweries, art galleries, forest lakes, spas, yoga retreats and farm stays. With so much to look forward to, including a beachside apartment, we made plans for an early morning getaway. Despite the early alarm and frantic dash to pack the cars, we soon found ourselves in heavy traffic.

As Alan and his family followed in their hired car, it seemed to me that the residents of Perth were on a mass exodus towards the south. All kinds of contraptions were being towed, including boats and caravans of every size and shape. During a rare chance to overtake, we passed many SUVs, all with trailers attached. Some were filled with children's bikes, beach balls, inflatables, camping chairs and tents. Others had fishing rods, surfboards, portable cookers and scooters.

The trip was meant to take three hours but took longer, because of toilet stops and a long queue for takeaway pies at a service station. While approaching the city of Bunbury, we passed a giant billboard depicting a picturesque harbour filled with anchored yachts. The setting looked idyllic, with large words scrolled across the bottom. *Welcome to Bunbury–You should see us now.*

A few cars took the turn for the city, but most veered left, towards Margaret River, Busselton and Dunsborough. Some vehicles peeled away 30 minutes later, towards the coastal town of Busselton, with its family-friendly beaches and timber-piled jetty that stretches far into the Indian Ocean. We kept on moving and came to a junction that split the traffic into two, either towards Margaret River or Dunsborough.

We chose the right turn, towards Dunsborough and drove along a stretch of road fringed either side by peppermint trees, home to the critically endangered western ringtail possum. To our right the ocean could be seen, twinkling between gaps in the trees or lapping against the sand. Soon after, we passed a stretch of beachside houses, each with expansive views across the sparkling waters of Geographe Bay.

By the time we arrived at our holiday home, the thermometer had nudged into the thirties and Fran had run out of entertainment ideas for Noah. Once free, he chased after a nearby gull and then spotted the ocean between a gap in the trees. After a quick change of clothes in the car park, he ran with Blake towards the beach. Soon they were splashing happily, as the adults stood barefoot in the shallows, contemplating sunset drinks and a barbeque.

Before us lay the calm waters of Geographe Bay, dotted with family-sized boats. I stared at the glistening water, trying to work out what shade of blue it was. Turquoise maybe, or a vibrant emerald. It was clear enough to see to the bottom, and as we walked along the shoreline, schools of tiny fish darted in and out of view.

Soon after, a lone paddleboarder appeared on the scene, standing tall, with gentle strokes that carved through the mirror-like surface. She was close to shore, heading from left to right, and waved to us while passing by. Overhead, the sun blazed in a perfect sky, with no hint of a cloud to be seen. As if on cue, three pelicans glided past, their wings outstretched as they made a final turn before landing on the water. I'd only been in Dunsborough for ten minutes and was already hooked.

As with all memorable holidays, the week flew by. During this time, we enjoyed lunch at a winery, watched surfers in action and took a walk along part of the Cape-to-Cape track. This is one of Australia's longest coastal walks, stretching 135 kilometres from Cape Naturaliste to Cape Leeuwin, where the Indian Ocean gives way to the Southern Ocean. Those who venture along the track get the chance to walk through karri forests, or to spend time on long sandy beaches far from the crowds. We chose a section of track that led us onto limestone cliffs, for the chance to view the ocean from up high.

It was out of season for whale watching, but we still took the time to search for signs of life in the water. No whales, but we spotted a line of surfers on a bush track, boards balanced on heads, strolling to a secret spot.

Deep in the karri forests, you'll find trees that are over two hundred years old. Some reach as tall as 90 metres and a select few were once chosen by fire wardens as natural lookout towers. They pegged the trunks with metal rods, to form a spiral staircase stretching from the forest floor to the canopy. Tree houses were then constructed in the upper branches, to enable spotters to stand in comfort while observing the forest.

Some of these trees are still accessible to climb, and during our week away I took a drive with Fran and Noah to investigate. It took two hours, mainly through farmland and pockets of woodland, until we came to a turning for Warren National Park. The bitumen soon gave way to compacted dirt, as we drove alongside majestic trees that seemed to reach up to the passing clouds.

We paused at a wooden hut manned by a warden. He looked to be in his late fifties and wore a green cotton shirt and matching shorts. He'd been reading a book, which he set to one side while collecting the entrance fee and handing over an admission slip. 'Here you go, sir. This is your daily pass. We don't allow overnight stays unless you're in one of the designated camping spots.'

To put him at ease, I said, 'Thanks mate. We're just here for an hour or two. I'm keen to find one of the climbing trees, as—'

He smiled and casually pointed towards a turn in the dirt road. 'Well, you're in luck, as the nearest one is just around the corner and you're the first car in ages. There's no one else around unless a few trekkers appear, but in this heat, I doubt it.'

As I stowed the admission slip and complimentary map, he continued to talk. 'The one nearby is supposedly the tallest climbing tree in the world. Are you planning to photograph it or climb it?'

'I'm not sure. Maybe both. Is it hard to climb?'

'How would I know? I've never done it. There are 165 pegs and no-one has fallen off yet, but that doesn't mean it's easy.'

'Is there a guide, or ropes or—'

'No, mate. You'll be on your own. It's just a set of metal pegs that go around in a spiral until you reach a couple of steep ladders to take you to the lookout point at 65 metres. There are no ropes or harnesses. All you need is common sense and a head for heights.'

Just before I drove away, he called out, 'If you fall off, just remember there's no phone reception around here.'

With that, he went back to his book, and we went in search of a very tall tree! The first thing I noticed when we got out of the car was the prolific bird life. Some sounded like playful monkeys, with their high-pitched screeches–others flew past in a flash of colour. Fran spotted a bright blue wren, no bigger than a mouse, darting from tree to tree. A flock of inquisitive parrots swooped from the trees to forage close to our feet. They might have been expecting a feed, but we had little to offer, except a few seeds and crumbs from a leftover sandwich.

Fran knelt with Noah and offered the remains in an open palm. Within seconds, a green-and-yellow bird perched on her hand, pecking at the morsels. With such a meagre offering, it didn't take long and with nothing more to offer, Fran lifted her arm to tempt the bird to fly. It responded with a friendly chirp, and flew away, in search of richer pickings.

Noah was the first to spot the climbing tree and ran towards the wide trunk. I tried calculating how many adults could stand around it, with their arms stretched wide to touch the next in line. Maybe five or six I figured, although it was hard to concentrate while estimating the height of the tree using imperial measurements. If the canopy stretched 250 feet, the wooden platform was roughly 200 feet from the ground, which meant the same height as 15 double-decker buses stacked on top of each other!

While craning hard to locate the platform, I heard Fran chatting to Noah about the local wildlife. He seemed more interested in the metal pegs spiralling around the trunk and took a bold move towards the first one. Fran held him tight as he took his first step and contemplated the next in line, but the gap proved too wide for such little legs. His time would come later in life! After a glug of water, I stepped onto the first rung and said, 'Here goes. Only 164 left to go.'

Fran gave a mischievous grin and asked, 'Why are you going first, instead of me?'

'I didn't think—'

She waved me away with a knowing smile. 'I used to climb trees when I was a kid, as well! Go on, up you go and enjoy yourself. I might have a try after you. Don't forget to hang on tight and wave from the top.'

And with that, I ruffled Noah's hair and set off on a solo trip around the outside of the tree. As I climbed the seemingly endless steps, a few thoughts came to mind regarding the safety barrier positioned outside the pegs. It resembled the kind of chicken wire purchased at hardware stores, and I doubted its resilience if anything heavy fell against it. I'd already noticed one slight opening, which had peeled away with age.

I was also concerned about slipping through the sizeable gaps between each foothold. Each narrow rung seemed to be placed at a different angle and spacing to the last. Sometimes they were close together, but in a few places the distance had been far enough to make me falter. Down below, the only thing to stop my fall would be a collision with a lower peg or the questionably secure chicken wire. Such a fall could lead to broken bones, blood and gore. And there was no mobile phone coverage!

I needed to stop overthinking and get into a rhythm. This was helped in part by Noah. I could hear his little voice, calling out, 'Go Daddy,' as he stood at the base of the tree. I sensed that Fran also had high hopes that I'd accomplish the climb, due to the number of times I'd tried rock climbing. But I'd never been a bold climber. Mostly, I'd been secured by a rope while being helped to the top of steep crags by my best friend, Steve.

But he was back in England, and I was partway up the tallest climbing tree in the world, trying to stop my knees from shaking. I took a deep breath, steadied myself, and reached out for the next peg. As I did so, it moved in its slot! Ignoring the frantic voices in my head, I pulled on the loose peg and reached for the next. This one held firm and so did the next few, but I was unaware of the natural obstacle that lay ahead.

After a few more circuits and many more metres of ascent, instead of another metal rod to step on, I came across something much wider. It was a mottled branch, protruding from the tree at right angles. On closer inspection, the branch felt smooth to touch after years of foot traffic and offered little in the way of grip.

Alone and afraid, I shook my head in astonishment and tried to sum up the situation. This had to be the most dangerous tourist attraction in Australia, yet there were no disclaimer forms to fill in–no friendly guides to offer advice–no ropes to hold on to–and no adrenaline junkies waiting in line. It was just me–halfway up the tallest climbing tree in the world–holding on for dear life!

The next step I took was the most careful of my life, as I placed my foot on the centre of the branch before letting it take my weight. I then placed the other foot alongside it while stretching for the next available peg, my clammy hands grasping the rung in desperation. Throughout the manoeuvre, my heart pounded at the thought of what lay below. On a wet or windy day, such a location would be precarious or deadly, and with these thoughts in mind I gingerly stepped off the branch.

The next peg came easily and so did the next, but a noise from below stopped me in my tracks. I could hear male voices, getting nearer by the second. I looked down and spotted movement as two heads came into view. By the time the two men caught me up, I was within sight of the wooden platform. Throughout their climb, they nattered away in French, as though walking alongside each other on a beach, not high above the forest floor, with nothing but chicken wire to stop their fall.

As they passed me by, I stayed close to the trunk, which forced them wide against the safety mesh. They looked to be in their early twenties, with tanned faces and chirpy smiles. They said hello in English, before switching back to French and continuing their journey. I followed close behind and watched as they climbed a steep metal ladder onto the platform. I arrived soon after, clambering through an open hatch onto a wooden deck 65 metres from the forest floor.

Still kneeling, I let out a sigh of relief and caught sight of the two men standing in a corner, taking photos of the view. After catching my breath, I walked towards the guard rail and stared across the forest to faraway dunes. The last time I'd seen so many trees together had been while working as a conservation volunteer in the jungles of Ecuador. There were no monkeys this time or butterflies floating by. But there was a sense of peace, with just a gentle breeze to stir the leaves.

Before they left the lookout point, the men asked me to take a photo of them together, side by side, with a backdrop of trees and passing clouds. Afterwards, I asked if they were on holiday. In near-perfect English, they told me about their campervan trip from Perth to Margaret River and their dream to go surfing. They were now headed to Esperance, on the south coast. The taller of the two seemed to be the chattiest, and as his friend gestured to leave, he stopped by the open hatch. 'I hear they have kangaroos on the beach at Esperance, which sounds kind of cool. Then we will head across the Nullarbor, towards Adelaide and Sydney. If we have enough time and money, maybe we will make it all the way to Byron Bay.'

I wished them good luck and watched as they eased themselves off the platform. Suddenly, I was alone and could hear my name being called from afar. I walked to the edge and peered over the side. Fran had moved into a clearing, with Noah on her shoulders. They looked almost antlike from so far away, but I thought I could make out Noah waving. I took a deep breath and shouted as loud as I could. 'Hello Noah. Hello Fran. Hello world!'

While waiting for a reply, a red-tailed black cockatoo flew past, its screeching calls echoing over the forest canopy. I stood in silence and watched the endangered bird skimming above the trees, fading from sight with every beat of its blackened wings. Now it was my time to take flight. Without looking down, I edged towards the ladder and muttered, 'Only 65 metres to go, including one loose rung and a slippery branch.'

On our final evening, we took a stroll along the beach to watch anglers cast their lines into the bay, in the hope of a feed of herring. As the sun dropped towards the wooded ridgeline, I turned to Fran and said, 'That's the end of the day and the end of another year. I wonder what next year will bring us?'

'Who knows, Alistair?' she said. 'Hopefully we'll get back to the forest, and it'll be my turn to get to the top of that tree!'

By the following morning, we were packed up and ready to head back to Perth. To take advantage of the late check out, I took a walk with Fran and Noah into the town centre, taking in the mid-morning sunshine as residents and holidaymakers came to life. The bakery was enjoying a roaring trade, and we joined a queue for pies, coffee and juices, as the aroma of baked bread filled the air. We took our takeaway treats to a nearby park and searched for a shady spot amongst the gum trees.

While Noah fed crumbs to the resident gulls, joggers came and went, along with dog walkers, cyclists, kids on scooters and mums pushing buggies. Just before we left, I heard shrieks of laughter, as three youngsters cycled into view, each carrying foam body boards. After leaning their bikes and boards against a tree, they set off to the bakery without a backward glance, merrily chatting along the way.

They returned soon after, with chips, pies and cold drinks, and sat in a circle. Fran noticed me studying them and gave me a nudge. 'Penny for your thoughts, Ali?'

I smiled and said, 'Look at those lads. They don't seem to have a care in the world. They left their bikes without a worry and are now contemplating which surf spot to try next.'

A man on a nearby bench overheard me and joined in with the conversation. He looked to be in his mid-thirties, with sun-bleached hair and an easy-going smile. He pointed to the boys and said, 'My son is the one in the middle and I agree, they have a good life here. Mind you, even in such a family friendly town, you have to be careful with bikes and boards going missing, especially during the summer when the place goes nuts.'

I soon learned that he lived nearby and earned a living by flying north to stay in an iron ore mining camp for weeks at a time, driving a haul truck capable of carrying 200 tonnes of lucrative red dirt. He was now on a week-long break but didn't want to venture too far from home, due to all the holiday traffic. He then explained about life in the town. 'The southwest goes crazy a few times a year, around Christmas and Easter. Other than that, it's a cool place to live, especially if you like the outdoors. There are no big shopping centres nearby, which suits me just fine.'

As he stood to leave, he smiled down at Noah. 'It's a great place to raise children, especially if you can get them into sport. My boy has grown up learning to surf and is a bit of a free spirit. Within a few years, he'll be out with his mates, camping in the bush.'

The man had more to say and leaned closer. 'Mind you, it's not all blue skies, surfing and fishing. The weather can be cold in winter, with far too much wind and rain for my liking. If you come back on a wet Wednesday in July, you'll think you've stepped into a ghost town.'

After thanking the man, we returned to our accommodation and as I loaded up the car, Fran diverted to the reception desk. When I next saw her, she handed over a colourful leaflet depicting a surfboard and nodded towards Noah, who was munching grapes while strapped in his seat. 'It looks like surfing lessons start at an early age in these parts. In a few years' time, he could be out on the water.'

While smiling at the thought, I picked a grape from Noah's lap and stole one last look around the grounds. Ninety minutes later, while in convoy with Alan, Sam and Blake, we passed a sign by the side of the road: *Thank you for visiting the southwest. Please drive safely. We hope to see you again.*

Our friends flew back to the UK a week later, with tears and hugs at Perth airport. The holiday had opened their eyes to the beauty of Western Australia, and I sensed they were keen to return. After waving them goodbye, I spotted a taxi driver outside the terminal waiting for a fare and thought back to our arrival in Melbourne a few years earlier.

We'd flown in from Fiji after securing visas from the Australian consulate and had taken a taxi to the city. At the time, we had no idea where to visit next and had asked for his advice. He'd mentioned a place called Ningaloo Reef, renowned as one of the last remaining great ocean paradises. It is Australia's longest fringe reef, stretching 300 kilometres along the northwest coast and home to an abundance of marine life including turtles, sharks and over 500 species of fish.

I felt the time was approaching when we'd finally take a visit, although our wish-list of places to explore also included a trip to the Northern Territory to experience Kakadu National Park, dual listed by UNESCO for its outstanding natural and cultural values. It is Australia's largest national park, covering an area half the size of Switzerland.

Instead of snow-capped mountains, it has rivers, floodplains, gorges and vast tracts of savannah. It is home to over 10,000 crocodiles and has been inhabited by Aboriginal people for 65,000 years, making it the oldest living culture on earth. In contrast to the wilds of Kakadu, we were also keen to head east by campervan, for a road trip from Sydney to Byron Bay, the coastal surf town renowned for its laid-back vibe.

But first we needed a base camp–somewhere to call home, away from the city and close to nature. Back in our car, I reached for a map of Australia and skimmed through the pages, contemplating the months and years ahead, following the sun on our next adventures in a land Down Under.

Bring me Sunshine:
More Bite-Sized Travels across a Sunburned Country

"Before us lay a road into no man's land–filled with rivers, gorges and vast tracts of open plains. Far on the horizon, a shimmering haze gave few clues to what lay beyond, as the tropical sun beat down on a parched land, begging for rain. After cranking the air conditioning, I called out a warning to the kids to watch out for crocodiles, snakes and kangaroos. We were heading into the wild!"

Join travel writer Alistair McGuinness as he embarks on more bite-sized adventures across Australia, including a campervan trip from Sydney to the hipster paradise of Byron Bay. Armed with a curious nature and a desire to enjoy each new experience, these travels also lead him into the wilds, foraging for bush tucker with an Aboriginal guide, before diving into the crystal-clear waters of Ningaloo Reef.

Each new adventure offers something different, from the vast iron ore mines of the Pilbara to the wild beauty of Monkey Mia, famed for its bottle-nosed dolphins. Along the way, Alistair encounters nomads, tourists and friendly locals, each with a tale to tell about their travels in Australia. If you enjoy travel stories, this fun-filled memoir will have you reaching for a map of Australia and planning your own adventures as you immerse yourself in the wonders of a land Down Under. With each turn of the page, you'll be transported to a place where the beers are cold, the days are sunny, and the open road stretches forever.

Postcards from South America:
A Pig in a Taxi, Cotopaxi and Two Sticks of Dynamite

After losing his job, Alistair took the plunge and travelled into the wilds of South America with his wife. Months later, they were running for their lives in Bolivia!

Join Alistair and Fran as they raft down the Amazon, teach English in the jungle, climb volcanoes and endure a hair-raising taxi ride across the Andes, along with a pig! Before tackling the Inca trail, they hired a donkey called Angus and trekked across a remote mountain pass, with just a mud map to guide them.

While venturing off the beaten track, they discovered Inca ruins, bustling markets and mountain villages inhabited by kindly folk offering food and shelter. If you enjoy fun-filled travel stories, *Postcards from South America* will tempt you to reach for a map, pack your bags and take the trip you've always dreamed about!

Wild About Africa:

Sleepwalking on Kilimanjaro and Running from Lions

Take a seat up front on an overland truck for the best view of Africa, following a journey from Kilimanjaro to Cape Town. During Alistair's first week, he came face to face with a marauding hyena. It didn't help that he was barefoot, in boxer shorts and a T-shirt, while in the wilds of the Serengeti. Soon after, he was robbed of all his possessions.

Luckily, he loaned a pair of pink tracksuit pants and a baggy Arran jumper, to wear while climbing Kilimanjaro, the highest freestanding mountain in the world. If you've ever wondered what it's like to drive across the Ngorongoro Crater on a dawn safari, touch the snows of Kilimanjaro, go quad biking across the Namib Desert or visit the prison that once held Nelson Mandela, this fun packed story is just the ticket for an inspirational adventure.

End to End:

John O'Groats, Broken Spokes and a Dog called Gretna

When three friends set off on a 900-mile trip to explore Britain, using an out of date map to guide them, the scene is set for a wayward adventure. One cyclist didn't own a bike, but luckily, his brother was working out of town and had one in his garage. Painted racing green, with wide wheels and a robust frame, it was far from perfect for such a trip. But it was free!

Along the way they visited numerous country pubs, went in search of the remaining Beatles, discovered an ancient hideaway used by Scottish clans, and survived a storm in the Highlands. Each time they got lost they were helped by a variety of kind and quirky characters.

If you like adventure travel books, then you'll enjoy this tale about three ordinary men, proving that extraordinary things can happen, just when you least expect it. For one of the cyclists, the journey would change his life forever.

Slow Down and Enjoy the Ride

Is it possible to cycle 1,000 miles across Britain in 13 days and still find the time to slow down and enjoy the ride? Twenty years after riding from Land's End to John O'Groats, Alistair set out with his friends to repeat the adventure and quickly discovered that times have changed. Bike computers have replaced maps and thousands of cycle paths now criss-cross Britain. It didn't help that he now lives in Australia and spends more time on a paddleboard than two wheels.

With little training and a borrowed bike, he set off from Land's End, determined to enjoy every moment. Faced with so many natural distractions, he soon began deviating from the plan. With many miles to cover along remote tracks, these diversions came at a price and something had to break. Would it be the bike, the camaraderie or Alistair's inquisitive nature?

Along the way he survived heatstroke in Devon, went in search of a lady called Daphne, and braved wild storms in Glasgow. After a swim in Loch Ness, he found time to enjoy a beer in one of the remotest pubs in Scotland. Everyone who travels across Britain has a story to tell. This is Alistair's.

If you like travel books, you'll enjoy this inspirational story, which shows that with luck, curiosity and perseverance, anything is possible.

Acknowledgements

This book is dedicated to my wife, Fran. I am in debt for her guidance and support, helping to turn scribbles from a travel diary into words in a book. Thanks also to the following cafés and coffee shops, who have supplied nibbles and drinks while I've been tapping away on my laptop during weekends or early mornings over many years.

Brewalicious, Busselton

Shelter Brewing Co, Busselton

The Good Egg, Busselton

The Urban Coffee House, Busselton

Tonic by the Bay, Busselton

I enjoy keeping in touch with readers and you can find me at the following locations:

On my website @ alistairmcguinness.com

On Facebook @ alistairmcguinnesswriter

On Instagram @ alistair_mcguinness

I've recently started a Podcast, called *A Taste of Australia*, where I get the chance to chat with travel enthusiasts who have a story to tell about their journeys in Australia. Come and pay a visit sometime, or maybe consider being a guest–while sharing your own travel stories about Australia.

Happy travels,

Alistair

Printed in Great Britain
by Amazon

42133545R00126